I0833427

NEVER
SAY
IT!

Never Say It!

The Words That Hold You Back and What to Say Instead

Judy Selby

Cris Cawley

Published by Game Changer Publishing

Scripture Disclaimer: Scripture quotations throughout this book are taken from various translations of the Bible. Unless otherwise indicated, passages may be quoted from multiple versions, including but not limited to the King James Version (KJV), New King James Version (NKJV), New International Version (NIV), and other widely recognized translations. All Scripture is used respectfully for purposes of commentary, reflection, and educational discussion.

Paperback ISBN: 979-8-90158-290-9

Hardcover ISBN: 979-8-90158-163-6

Digital ISBN: 979-8-90158-164-3

www.GameChangerPublishing.com

THE WORDS THAT HOLD
YOU BACK AND
WHAT TO SAY INSTEAD

JUDY SELBY & CRIS CAWLEY

CONTENTS

This book is dedicated to every person who has ever been shaped by the power of words.

May these pages serve as a reminder that our words carry weight. They can build or break, encourage or discourage, open doors or close them. Used with intention, they have the power to transform relationships, influence outcomes, and change lives, including our own.

To those committed to speaking with greater awareness, wisdom, and integrity, this book is for you.

READ THIS FIRST

Go here to learn more and connect with Cris and Judy

INTRODUCTION

Before I started law school, I worked in retail on 23rd Street in Manhattan. The store sat in the middle of the city's daily rhythm. Neighborhood residents dropped by, businesspeople rushed in on lunch breaks, and university students drifted in between classes. Registers beeped, doors swung open, and employees moved fast from one customer to the next, always trying to keep up with the pace of New York.

A few months after I started, we hired a new employee. He was really a great guy, and everyone genuinely liked him. But he had a peculiar habit. Every day, without fail, he would walk in through the front door and announce, "I'm so tired."

At first, we tried to understand. Did something happen the night before? Was he sick? Did he need help? But soon it became clear: this wasn't a request for sympathy; it was just what he said, every single day.

One morning, he walked in, headed straight toward a group of us, and repeated his familiar mantra: "I'm so tired."

And suddenly, something clicked. I watched the reaction sweep through the room, including the slump in shoulders, the quiet sighs, the yawning, and the subtle drain of energy among people who, moments earlier, had been moving with momentum. His words shifted the entire atmosphere. The whole room seemed to fall half a step behind.

It was such a downer.

In that moment, I realized I could not allow myself to have that kind of impact on others or on myself. I was never really like him, but that morning I made a decision: I would never say the words "I am tired" again.

That moment of clarity became the beginning of what would later grow into my *Never Say It* List. At first, it was a personal, instinctive response to negativity. But over time, it grew to include phrases like "I do not feel like it" and "I cannot." Slowly, it became a kind of code, a filter for language that either builds energy or drains it. It was not about perfection; it was about awareness. Words are more than sounds. They are actions shaping our world long before we realize it.

I first mentioned the Never Say It List in my book, *The Untold Secrets to Thrive as a Lawyer*, and the response surprised me. Lawyer or not, people saw themselves in it. And the more I heard from them, the more I realized this concept might be more than a chapter. It might be a book of its own.

That's when I began digging deeper.

I already knew scripture supported this principle. Verses about the power of the tongue, about life and death residing in our words, echoed in my mind. But I wondered whether science had reached the same conclusion. Could modern research confirm what faith had always taught, that the words we speak actually mold our experience of the world?

I began looking into the research, and what I found astonished me.

Study after study confirmed that language affects brain chemistry, focus, emotion, and behavior. Negative self-talk triggers neurological responses that increase fatigue and stress; positive speech encourages confidence, motivation, and resilience.

Science said what scripture had already declared: words have power.

Around that time, I reached out to Cris Cawley, the CEO of Game Changer Publishing, which had published my first book. I wanted her thoughts on transforming the Never Say It concept into its own project. The call was meant to last fifteen minutes, but it stretched on for nearly an hour. We shared the same conviction about the importance of self-talk and the words we speak to others. Cris's perspective, as both a CEO and a mom, added dimension to the idea. By the end of our conversation, we knew we were going to take this journey together.

Mastering self-talk and being cognizant of the words that come out of your mouth daily is not theory. It is practice, lived out by some of the most successful people in the world. Athletes like Serena Williams have spoken about the deliberate, positive self-talk used to maintain focus under pressure. Entrepreneurs like Richard Branson and Oprah Winfrey credit part of their success to how they frame challenges as opportunities and how intentionally they choose the words they speak to their teams and to themselves. Coaches, actors, and personal development leaders do this as well. They choose words that elevate those around them because they understand that energy is contagious and that language is one of the most powerful ways to transfer it.

In this book, you will discover scripture, science, and stories about how much your words really matter. Scripture reminds us that our words have power. Science shows us that this power is tangible, measurable, and transformative. And the stories of high achievers demonstrate how this principle plays out in the real world, shaping careers, relationships, and lives that might never have existed if negativity had been allowed to dominate their speech.

You will also find practical tactics you can use in your daily life. You will learn to recognize phrases that hold you back, replace them with empowering alternatives, and consciously choose words that energize and uplift.

Mastering this skill is not only about becoming your best self. It equips you to help others become their best, to unlock potential they did not know they had, and to build futures that once seemed out of reach.

The words you speak matter more than you realize. They shape your energy, your mindset, your relationships, your daily life, and the world around you. They can build people up or tear them down. They can open doors to possibilities you never imagined.

We invite you to explore this simple yet powerful concept while discovering how to use words to speak life and transform not only our own worlds but also the worlds of those around us.

1

WORDS ARE THE FOUNDATION OF YOUR LIFE

"The words 'I am' are potent words; be careful what you hitch to them. The thing you're claiming has a way of reaching back and claiming you."
– A.L. Kitselman

What we say becomes what we see. Our words shape our identity, influence our beliefs, and program our expectations.

Mel Robbins and Shonda Rhimes shared in a conversation on *The Mel Robbins Podcast* that the words we speak to ourselves function like a spell. They hold power, and the more we repeat them, the more real they become, whether for good or harm. Saying "yes" to things that scare us reveals the courage we already possess. Our internal language becomes a catalyst, expanding our sense of capability each time we choose to speak life and move forward.

The Bible speaks directly to this:

"As a man thinks in his heart, so is he" (Proverbs 23:7).

What we think often finds expression in what we say. Our words are the outward echo of our inner beliefs. Consider the principle of the self-fulfilling prophecy.

When we repeatedly say things like "I'm always late," "Things never work out for me," or "I'm terrible with money," we're not just making casual observations. We're actually reinforcing our identity. Once an identity takes root, our actions begin to align with it. But you don't have to take our word for it. Neuroscience supports this.

Brain imaging studies show that repeated thoughts, especially spoken ones, strengthen neural pathways. Over time, those pathways become our default patterns. If you constantly tell yourself you are not good enough, your brain begins to believe it, and then you behave accordingly. But the reverse is also true. When you start speaking life, confidence, and truth, your brain begins to accept a new identity.

Psychology Today notes that negative self-talk can lead to increased stress and depression, lower self-esteem, and a greater likelihood of giving up when faced with challenges. But there is hope. Studies show that positive affirmations can reduce stress, improve academic performance, and enhance resilience.

Consider Oprah Winfrey. In her early twenties, she was told she was unfit for television. At a Baltimore news station, she was demoted from her anchor desk job because she became too emotional when covering stories. Imagine hearing those words at the very beginning of your career, the kind of words that could crush a dream.

Most people would have accepted those words as truth. But Oprah did not. Instead, she reframed the story she told herself. She decided her emotional connection was not a weakness; it was her greatest strength. That shift in language changed the trajectory of her life. What others dismissed became the very thing that built one of the most successful and influential media empires of all time.

Her story reveals a timeless truth. Your words are not background noise. They are seeds. What you speak over yourself and others will eventually grow into reality.

Let's look at a few other examples.

Muhammad Ali

Born Cassius Clay in Louisville, Kentucky, Muhammad Ali grew up in a segregated America where young Black men were often told through both words and actions that their futures were limited. As a teenager, after his bicycle was stolen, a local police officer encouraged him to take up boxing. From that moment, Ali began training with fire in his spirit.

But what truly set him apart was not just his fists; it was his words. Long before he became a champion, Ali constantly declared, "I am the greatest." Reporters rolled their eyes. Opponents laughed. But Ali never stopped saying it. He was not simply bragging; he was programming himself to believe it.

> "It is the repetition of affirmations that leads to belief. And once that belief becomes a deep conviction, things begin to happen."

His affirmations became prophecies. Before his 1964 fight against the heavily favored Sonny Liston, Ali boldly predicted victory. He rhymed, he boasted, he said he would shock the world. And he did. At twenty-two years old, he became the heavyweight champion of the world, afterward shouting, "I shook up the world!"

Years later, in the legendary "Rumble in the Jungle" against George Foreman, Ali again used his words to shape reality. Foreman was considered unbeatable, a devastating puncher in his prime. But Ali declared he had a strategy, later called the "rope-a-dope." Round after round, he taunted Foreman with words. "Is that all you got, George? They told me you could hit." His words were weapons, disarming Foreman's confidence as much as his defense absorbed the blows. In the eighth round, Ali knocked Foreman out, reclaiming the heavyweight crown.

And of course, there was his famous mantra, "Float like a butterfly, sting like a bee. The hands can't hit what the eyes can't see." These were not just clever lines. They were verbal blueprints for how he would fight. He spoke them, he believed them, and then he embodied them.

Even in his later years, as Parkinson's disease weakened his body, the words "I am the greatest" still echoed. By then, his words were no longer just about boxing titles. They had become a legacy, inspiring millions to see themselves as more than the labels society put on them.

Ali's story shows us that your words do not just describe who you are. They create who you become, and over time, they can influence entire cultures.

Steve Jobs

In 1985, Steve Jobs was fired from Apple, the very company he co-founded. Most people would have been buried under words like "failure" and "rejected." But years later, Jobs reframed the moment in his famous Stanford commencement address:

"Getting fired from Apple was the best thing that could have ever happened to me. It freed me to enter one of the most creative periods of my life."

Notice the language. He redefined what others saw as ruin as opportunity. Out of that creative period came NeXT, Pixar, and eventually Apple's golden era, which gave us the iPod, iPhone, and iPad.

Jobs's story proves that the way you speak about your circumstances determines whether they bury you or build you.

Les Brown

Les Brown, one of the world's most influential motivational speakers, didn't begin his life with a microphone in his hand or an audience eager to hear his words. He began with a label.

As a child in Miami, Florida, Les was adopted along with his twin brother and raised by a single mother, Mamie Brown, who worked tirelessly as a cafeteria worker and domestic servant to provide for them. Though she lacked financial resources, she gave her sons fierce love, discipline, and encouragement. But outside the safety of home, young Les faced challenges that cut deeply.

In elementary school, after struggling with lessons and being held back a grade, a teacher wrote something on his record that would follow him for years: "educably mentally retarded." In today's terms, it meant the school believed he was slow, incapable of learning at the same pace as others. That label was stamped on his file and branded into his identity. Teachers repeated it. Students teased him with it. And Les, hearing it often enough, began to believe it.

One day in high school, when he was asked to work a problem on the chalkboard, Les nervously declined. "I can't do that," he told the teacher. "I'm educably mentally retarded."

He expected the teacher to nod in agreement, as so many others had.

But this teacher, Mr. Leroy Washington, stopped, turned to Les, and locked eyes with him. He refused to accept that excuse. "Don't you ever say that again," he said firmly. Then, leaning closer, he spoke words that pierced the label and planted something new: "Don't ever let someone else's opinion of you become your reality."

That single sentence broke through years of shame. For the first time, someone directly challenged the lie that had defined him. Mr. Washington treated him not as a failure but as a young man with untapped potential. From that moment forward, Les began to believe he could do more, be more, become more.

The road wasn't easy. He still struggled. He still faced setbacks. But the words of one teacher had awakened him. They gave him permission to dream.

He went on to pursue broadcasting and became a popular radio DJ known as "Les Brown, the man about town." Later, he entered politics, serving in the Ohio state legislature. Eventually, he found his true calling, speaking into the lives of others the very words that Mr. Washington spoke into his, words that shatter labels, words that awaken possibility, and words that create new realities.

Today, millions around the world know Les Brown as one of the greatest motivational speakers alive. His message is simple yet profound: "You have greatness within you." And it all traces back to a teacher who refused to let a young man be limited by someone else's opinion.

This story reminds us of an essential truth: children, spouses, friends, and even strangers carry labels. Some are spoken by others, some whispered by their own minds. But labels do not have the final word. Words of life can break them. One sentence, spoken with conviction, can reframe an identity and alter a destiny.

Just as Les Brown's life was changed forever, we, too, have the power to change the course of someone else's future simply by refusing to let them settle for a lie.

Maya Angelou

Maya Angelou's story is another clear example of how the right words, spoken at the right time, can literally awaken a voice that the world was meant to hear.

At seven years old, Maya endured a horrific trauma: she was assaulted by her mother's boyfriend. When she confessed to what had happened, her family took action, and shortly after, the man was killed.

Maya, only a child, came to believe that her words had

caused his death. She internalized the lie that her voice was dangerous, that speaking could bring destruction, so she stopped talking altogether.

For nearly five years, Maya was mute, communicating only through gestures, notes, and an occasional word spoken to her brother. To her family and teachers, she appeared locked inside herself, a little girl silenced by fear and shame.

But during this time of silence, Maya devoured books. She memorized poetry, studied the rhythms of language, and filled her imagination with the words of Shakespeare, Edgar Allan Poe, and Black literary voices such as Paul Laurence Dunbar. She was absorbing words, but wouldn't release them.

Then came Mrs. Bertha Flowers, an elegant, educated woman from the same small town where Maya was growing up. Mrs. Flowers noticed Maya's silence but sensed the brilliance beneath it. She invited the young girl to her home, served her cookies and tea, and began to speak to her with warmth and dignity. She read poetry aloud, reciting lines with power and expression, then looked at Maya and said something that would change her life:

"You do not love poetry, not until you speak it. Words mean more than what is set down on paper. It takes the human voice to infuse them with the shades of deeper meaning."

Mrs. Flowers gently but firmly challenged Maya to speak again, not to chatter endlessly, but to speak beauty, to let her voice carry life. At first, Maya resisted. But slowly, under Mrs. Flowers' encouragement, she began to recite poetry aloud. For the first time in years, words left her lips. The silence that had once been a prison began to break.

Those moments planted the seeds of a destiny Maya could not yet see. The girl who had once believed her voice could kill would become a woman whose voice would heal, inspire, and awaken nations. Maya Angelou went on to become one of the most celebrated poets, authors, and voices of the twentieth century. Her works, *I Know Why the Caged Bird Sings, Phenomenal*

Woman, and *Still I Rise*, gave language to the struggles and the triumphs of generations. She stood on national stages, recited poetry at a presidential inauguration, and inspired millions with words that carried fire, dignity, and grace.

And it all began because one woman refused to let her stay silent. One woman believed in her, spoke life into her, and reintroduced her to the power of the spoken word.

Ashley Graham

Ashley Graham grew up in Lincoln, Nebraska, far from the runways that would later make her famous. As one of the most recognizable models in the world today, she's credited with transforming the conversation around body image in fashion and popular culture. But early in her career, the message she received from the industry was anything but positive.

Agents told her she was "too big" to be successful, and critics labeled her body as a liability. Graham learned to fight back, not through anger but through words, the ones she spoke to herself. She began practicing self-affirmations, consciously replacing the inner criticism she'd internalized with kindness and humor. Her open embrace of body positivity became a movement that inspired millions of women to speak differently about themselves.

"Back fat, I see you popping over my bra today. But that's all right. I'm gonna choose to love you."

Lindsey Vonn

For Olympic skier Lindsey Vonn, positive words from someone else were the spark that changed everything. Born in Minnesota and raised in a ski-loving family, Vonn was driven from a young age, but even talent needs belief. When she was nine years old, she met her idol, Olympic gold medalist Picabo Street, at an autograph signing.

In what Vonn later described as a "ninety-second conversation," Street told her she could be great if she believed it. That sentence, simple but powerful, became a seed that took root. Vonn went on to become one of the most decorated alpine skiers in history, with eighty-two World Cup victories and multiple Olympic medals.

She often credits Street's words as the moment she realized that greatness was not just possible but expected of her.

"Picabo Street told me I could be great. I believed her."

Anthony Ramos

Actor and musician Anthony Ramos grew up in a working-class Puerto Rican family in Brooklyn, New York. He had dreams of performing but little exposure to the world of Broadway or professional music.

Before finding fame in *Hamilton* and *In the Heights,* Ramos worked multiple jobs and often questioned whether his dreams were realistic.

What shifted his perspective were the affirming words of mentors who saw something special in him, most notably Lin-Manuel Miranda, who cast him in *Hamilton* and encouraged him to own his identity and his voice. Ramos has said that hearing someone tell him, "You belong here," changed the way he spoke to himself.

That external validation became internal belief, fueling a career built on authenticity, vulnerability, and purpose.

"When someone says, 'I see you,' that changes everything."

John McAvoy

John McAvoy's story is perhaps the most dramatic of all. Once one of Britain's most wanted armed robbers, McAvoy grew up surrounded by crime and served time in high-security prisons. His life began to shift when a prison officer named Darren

Davis recognized his extraordinary athletic ability and encouraged him to channel his energy into sport instead of violence.

Those simple words of belief, "You could be great at this," ignited a transformation. While incarcerated, McAvoy began training obsessively, setting world records on the indoor rowing machine.

After his release, he rebuilt his life as an elite endurance athlete and motivational speaker. Today he works with at-risk youth, helping them find purpose through sport and self-discipline, all because one person chose to speak to his potential instead of his past.

"A prison guard believed in me before I believed in myself."

The Science Behind Speech

Modern research affirms what Scripture and these stories demonstrate: your brain believes your words.

Neuroplasticity is the brain's ability to change and rewire itself over time. For decades, scientists believed the brain was fixed after childhood, but we now know that your thoughts, habits, and words can physically reshape your brain. Every time you repeat a phrase, you are strengthening the neural pathway that phrase travels on. Like carving a deeper groove in a record, the more you play it, the easier it becomes for your brain to replay the same pattern.

Both faith and science point to the same truth: your words are not harmless. They are programming your brain, your body, and your future.

Your words become the blueprint for your future, whether it pertains to your career, your relationships, or your faith. Everything you've built begins with something you've said, either out loud or to yourself.

The good news is that you can dismantle what's negative and rebuild with truth and positivity. Below are some practical steps to get started:

1. Start a word audit. Spend a full day tracking your speech. What do you say to yourself when you make a mistake? What do you say when you achieve something? How do you speak about your life, work, or body?
2. Identify negative scripts. Look for repeated phrases like "I always mess this up" or "Nothing ever works out for me." These are clues to deeper beliefs.
3. Choose replacement phrases. Replace negative or toxic phrases with the truth. Instead of saying, "I'm so stupid," say, "I'm still learning." Instead of saying, "I'm always tired," try saying, "I'm restoring my energy."
4. Practice gratitude. Begin and end your day by naming three things you're grateful for. This isn't just some abstract concept; it helps train your mind to focus on what's positive rather than what's negative.

Words are not empty. They are seeds. Oprah reframed *unfit* into *authentic* and built an empire. Muhammad Ali declared greatness until the world believed it. Steve Jobs redefined *failure* as the *best thing* and changed the world. Les Brown shattered a label and inspired millions. Maya Angelou broke her silence and gave voice to a generation.

The same power lives in your mouth today. What harvest will your words create?

Reflection Questions:

- What is one sentence you often repeat to yourself, whether positive or negative? How has it shaped your actions?
- Which of the stories in this chapter resonated most with you, and why?

- If someone followed you for a week, what phrases would they hear most often from your mouth? What would those phrases reveal about your beliefs?
- What labels have been spoken over you that you may still be carrying? How can you begin to replace them with words of truth?

2

THE POWER OF WORDS: A BIBLICAL PERSPECTIVE

Long before psychologists and neuroscientists explored the impact of language, the Bible made a bold statement about it. Proverbs 18:21 tells us that *"death and life are in the power of the tongue."* The Scriptures are filled with guidance and warnings about our speech because words are not neutral; they carry significant weight. They shape our reality, reflect our hearts, and influence our destinies.

Words were the first tool God used for creation. Genesis 1:3 states, *"And God said, 'Let there be light,' and there was light."* God didn't create the universe with His hands; He spoke it into existence.

Since we are made in His image, it follows that our words also hold creative power. While we may not create galaxies, we do shape the environments around us at home, at work, and within our own minds.

Let's explore six biblical truths that illustrate the true power of our words and what they mean for our daily lives.

1. Words Can Bring Life or Death (Proverbs 18:21)

"The tongue can bring death or life; those who love to talk will reap the consequences."

Consider the last thing someone said to you that left a lasting impression. Was it a word of encouragement or criticism? Most of us can recall hurtful words from years, even decades, ago. Why is that? Because negative words, in particular, have enduring power. They embed themselves in our memories, affect our self-worth, and influence our decisions.

Let's look at the early story of American politician Ben Hooper. Born in Tennessee in the late 1800s, Ben carried the heavy stigma of being born out of wedlock. He often hid in shame due to the ostracism he and his mother experienced in their small town, where people openly speculated about his father. One day, Ben attended a sermon by a new preacher, then tried to leave unnoticed. However, as he walked out, the preacher stopped him, placed a hand on his shoulder, and asked, "Hello, young man. Who's your daddy?"

A hush fell over the crowd, waiting to hear Ben's response. The preacher, sensing the tension, quickly reassured Ben, saying, "Actually, I know who you are. The resemblance is very clear. You're a child of God."

That moment transformed Ben's life. He began to shed his shame and embrace his worth. Eventually, he grew up to become the governor of Tennessee. That one sentence not only changed his future but also impacted millions of people in his state.

We see echoes of this truth even today. Simone Biles, the most decorated gymnast in history, has openly shared how the words spoken into her life helped her rise above abandonment and foster care. When her adoptive parents affirmed her with words like "You are ours," "You are loved," and "You belong here," they gave her the foundation to soar.

Just like Ben, her future was reshaped by words of belonging and affirmation.

2. Words Can Cause Great Destruction (James 3:5–6)

"In the same way, the tongue is a small thing that makes grand speeches. But a tiny spark can set a great forest on fire. And among all the parts of the body, the tongue is a flame of fire. It is a whole world of wickedness, corrupting your entire body. It can set your whole life on fire, for it is set on fire by hell itself."

In the book of James, the tongue is compared to a spark that can set an entire forest ablaze. Words can ignite conflicts, end marriages, wound both children and adults, divide churches, and dismantle companies.

But most often, the damage starts small: one careless insult, one sarcastic comment, or one heated accusation. We've all been scorched by words, and if we're honest, we've all burned others as well.

The challenge lies in taking responsibility for the fires we start and learning to control those flames. Our words have eternal consequences. This isn't just about foul language or lies; it encompasses every flippant comment, every passive-aggressive jab, and every so-called joke that cuts someone deeply. Our words echo in eternity. Gossip, slander, and complaining may seem insignificant, but they erode trust and breed division.

In 1963, Dr. Martin Luther King Jr. stood before 250,000 people at the Lincoln Memorial. Setting aside his notes, he spoke the words that still echo today:

"I have a dream… that my four little children will one day live in a nation where they will not be judged by the color of their skin but by the content of their character."

Those words galvanized a movement, painted a vision, and offered hope to millions. Words can divide, but they can also unite and heal.

In 2020, during the global pandemic, New Zealand's Prime Minister Jacinda Ardern addressed her nation with calm, empathetic words: "Be strong. Be kind. We are in this together." While some leaders fueled fear, her words created safety and collective responsibility. Research later showed her speeches increased national trust and unity.

3. Words Can Heal or Harm (Proverbs 12:18; 15:4)

"Gentle words are a tree of life; a deceitful tongue crushes the spirit."

"Some people make cutting remarks, but the words of the wise bring healing."

Gentle words are depicted as a tree of life, while harsh words are like sword thrusts. The Bible uses powerful imagery because this is a daily battle. Are your words nurturing the people around you or wounding them?

Further, our words should build up, not corrupt. Paul instructs that our words should be helpful, building others up according to their needs. Imagine the shift if every workplace, home, and school adopted this standard. What if, before speaking, we asked ourselves: *Will this build up or break down? Will it bless or burden? Will it help or hurt?*

Consider actor Ke Huy Quan, who starred as a child in *Indiana Jones and the Temple of Doom* and *The Goonies*. For decades, Hollywood told him there were no roles for Asian actors like him. He nearly gave up on his dream. But in 2022, a director believed in him, spoke life into his talent, and cast him in *Everything Everywhere All at Once*. At the Oscars, through tears, he declared, "Mom, I just won an Oscar!"

Words of encouragement resurrected a career once thought finished.

Words can crush dreams, or they can revive them.

4. Words Reflect the Heart (Luke 6:45)

"Out of the abundance of the heart, the mouth speaks."

Jesus said our speech is a mirror. If our words are consistently critical, negative, or sarcastic, the problem is not our vocabulary. It is our heart.

Our words reveal what is inside us. If we want to change our speech, we must first allow God to transform our hearts.

This is why athletes like Steph Curry are intentional about what they say. Curry, widely regarded as one of the greatest shooters in NBA history, has a habit of encouraging his teammates out loud. Coaches say his humble positivity changes the entire locker room.

The same can be said about NCAA Division I scoring champ Caitlin Clark. Before games, she makes a point of telling her teammates that they're amazing, reminding them that she believes in them. It's a small ritual, but one that speaks volumes about her leadership and how she uses her voice to build confidence in others.

That message has become such a signature part of Caitlin's approach that it is even inscribed on her own signature basketball: *You're amazing*.

It's more than a catchphrase. It's a reminder of the immense power of speaking positivity into those around you.

5. Words Shape Faith (Mark 11:23)

"I tell you the truth, you can say to this mountain, 'May you be lifted up and thrown into the sea,' and it will happen. But you must really believe it will happen and have no doubt in your heart."

Jesus said that if we speak in faith, even to mountains, they will move. This isn't merely poetic; it's a call to live expectantly. Our faith is activated by our words. Doubt can kill dreams, but bold, faith-filled speech brings them to life.

Let's revisit a few figures from the last chapter.

Muhammad Ali famously declared, "I am the greatest," long before the world believed him. His words shaped his identity, and his identity shaped his destiny.

Oprah Winfrey was told she was unfit for television. Instead of accepting those words, she reframed them. Her emotional connection became her greatest strength. That belief reshaped her career and ultimately an entire industry.

Steve Jobs, fired from Apple in 1985, could have spoken only of failure. Instead, he called it "the best thing that ever happened to me." That reframing turned rejection into fuel for innovation.

More recently, NFL quarterback Jalen Hurts, overlooked in college and doubted in the pros, has repeated one simple phrase: "I had a purpose before everyone else had an opinion." He spoke faith into his journey, and in just a few years, he led the Philadelphia Eagles to a Super Bowl appearance.

Words of faith do not deny reality. They declare possibility.

6. Words Build or Break Communities (Ephesians 4:29)

"Don't use foul or abusive language. Let everything you say be good and helpful, so that your words will be an encouragement to those who hear them."

Paul instructs that our words should be helpful, building others up according to their needs. Imagine the shift if every workplace, home, and school adopted this standard. What if, before speaking, we asked ourselves: *Will this build up or break down? Will it bless or burden? Will it help or hurt?*

Imagine homes, workplaces, and churches where this was the standard. Gossip would die. Criticism would fade. Encouragement would thrive. Communities would grow healthier and stronger.

We saw this during the 2018 Thai cave rescue, when twelve boys and their soccer coach were trapped underground for eighteen days. International rescuers repeatedly told the boys, "You are strong. You are not alone. We will get you out." Those words of hope carried them through impossible fear until every single one was rescued.

Words do not just impact us. They shape us.

Your words carry the same power. They can transform your child, heal your spouse, inspire a coworker, or even change the way you see yourself. Every sentence you speak is a seed.

What kind of legacy will your words plant?

Reflection Questions:

- What is the most life-giving sentence someone has ever spoken to you? How did it shape your life?
- What is the most destructive sentence someone has spoken to you? Are you still carrying it today?
- What words do you say often to yourself, your family, or your colleagues? Are they life-giving or destructive?
- Who in your life most needs words of encouragement right now? How could you give it to them this week?

3

THE SCIENCE BEHIND OUR SPOKEN WORDS

Modern science now validates what faith has always understood. From neuroscience to psychology to public health, a single truth is clearly emerging: words don't just affect emotions; they shape our reality. Every sentence you speak, hear, or think activates a complex network of biological processes. Words influence hormone levels, stimulate specific regions of the brain, and can alter your heart rate and immune function. Your words are active agents of change, capable of either healing or harm.

Science is proving what Scripture has said: *"Pleasant words are a honeycomb, sweet to the soul and healing to the bones"* (Proverbs 16:24). The phrase *"The tongue has the power of life and death"* (Proverbs 18:21) represents more than a spiritual principle. It is a measurable biological fact.

Let's examine what science is now confirming about the power of the spoken word.

1. The 7-38-55 Rule of Communication

Psychologist Dr. Albert Mehrabian found that emotional meaning is conveyed seven percent through words, thirty-eight percent through tone of voice, and fifty-five percent through body language. This does not diminish the importance of words; it magnifies their significance. If your tone and posture contradict your words, your message gets lost and distorted. Speaking life requires alignment, not just in what we say, but also in how we say it.

2. How Words Shape the Brain

The human brain is constantly rewiring itself, a phenomenon known as neuroplasticity. Every thought or phrase we repeat becomes a well-worn walking path. The more often we walk it, the more natural it becomes until it forms a well-worn road.

Psychologist Donald Hebb summarized this principle with the phrase, "Neurons that fire together, wire together." If you constantly say, "I always mess this up," your brain will create a well-worn road of failure. But if you say, "I am learning and improving," your brain will pave a pathway of resilience and persistence.

This is why athletes, business leaders, and high achievers train their words as carefully as they train their skills. Words create grooves in the brain that determine how we respond under pressure.

3. Words and Emotional Pain

FMRI brain scans show that emotionally charged words, especially negative ones, activate the amygdala, the brain's fear center, and the anterior cingulate cortex, which is linked to emotional pain.[1] In a 2019 study, participants exposed to pain-related words reported greater distress even without any physical injury. Their brains processed those words almost as if they had been physically harmed.

This is why an insult can feel like a gut punch, while encouragement feels like medicine. Your body is responding to the chemistry your words unleash.

4. Words and Stress Hormones

In the landmark study "Do Words Hurt?" Maria Richter and her team found that negative words trigger the release of cortisol, the stress hormone. Repeated phrases like "I cannot do this" or "I hate my life" create a flood of chemicals that weaken the immune system, disrupt sleep, and increase the risk of depression.[2]

On the other hand, positive words increase dopamine, which fuels motivation, and oxytocin, which builds trust and bonding. Encouraging words are not just nice. They are biochemical interventions that calm anxiety, sharpen focus, and strengthen relationships.

5. Words and Performance: Athletes as Proof

Nowhere is the science of words more visible than in the world of athletics. From playgrounds to Olympic podiums, self-talk often makes the difference between success and failure.

Sports psychologists have long documented the connection. Negative self-talk raises cortisol levels, tightens muscles, and increases the likelihood of mistakes. Conversely, positive self-talk calms the nervous system, increases focus, and boosts confidence.

Michael Phelps, the most decorated Olympian in history, did not just train his body; he also trained his words. Phelps visualized perfect races while repeating affirmations. By the time he stood on the starting blocks, his brain had already rehearsed winning thousands of times.

Serena Williams also leaned on self-talk throughout her career. In championship moments, she constantly repeated to herself, "I am strong. I can do this." Those words calmed her heartbeat, stabilized her breathing, and helped her deliver under pressure.

Even professionals rely on intentional language. Two-time NBA Most Valuable Player Giannis Antetokounmpo, who grew up in poverty in Greece, reframes disappointment with one line: "It is not failure. It is steps to success." Those words are not just for him. They model resilience for every young fan listening.

From Little League fields to the NBA, athletes prove that words set the stage for performance.

6. Words and Community

The ripple effects of words stretch beyond individuals to entire communities.

A University of Pennsylvania study analyzed millions of tweets across U.S. counties and found that language predicted health outcomes. Communities where posts were filled with sarcasm, anger, and hostility had significantly higher rates of heart disease. Communities where words like "joy," "hope," and "gratitude" were common had lower rates. Astonishingly, language patterns predicted disease rates more accurately than traditional risk factors like smoking or income.[3]

Workplaces show the same truth. A Gallup survey revealed that sixty-five percent of American workers had received no recognition in the past year. The absence of affirming words led to low morale, burnout, and high turnover. In contrast, employees who regularly heard encouragement were forty-five percent less likely to quit.[4]

Words did not just impact culture. They affected the bottom line.

7. Words and Children

Children's brains are uniquely sensitive to the language spoken over them. A study at MIT found that positive verbal interaction between adults and children increased activity in areas of the brain linked to language processing and executive function. Encouragement literally helps children's brains grow stronger.[5]

NBA star Giannis Antetokounmpo's story illustrates this well. Before he became a champion, he was a boy selling trinkets on the streets of Athens to help his family survive. His mother often told him, "You will make it. You will be great." Today, his resilience and confidence echo those life-giving words.

Parents, teachers, and mentors should take note early on. Every phrase spoken to a child is shaping not only their confidence but also their brain development, future outlook, and perspective on life.

8. Words and Perception of Reality

Language shapes how we perceive reality itself. Linguists call this semantic prosody, the emotional tone carried by words.

For example:

- Saying "He is unemployed" suggests defeat.
- Saying "He is seeking opportunities" suggests progress.

Both statements may be factually accurate, but they create entirely different realities in the mind.

This is why leaders use framing intentionally. Calling a challenge a *problem* creates paralysis. Calling it an *opportunity* ignites creativity. Words shape whether people freeze in fear or lean into innovation.[6]

Proverbs 16:24 says, *"Pleasant words are a honeycomb, sweet to the soul and healing to the bones."* Research now shows that encouraging speech lowers stress, boosts immunity, and fosters resilience. Proverbs 18:21 tells us, *"The tongue has the power of life and death."*

Science confirms it. Your words are programming your brain, influencing your body, and shaping your future.

Every sentence is a seed. The question is whether you are planting weeds or fruit.

Words Have Power, Especially the Ones You Aim at Yourself

Dr. Daniel Amen, a prominent psychiatrist and founder of Amen Clinics, has devoted his career to showing how our thoughts and words literally shape the health of our brains. His work makes clear that the language we use is not neutral. Words are powerful tools that can build us up or tear us down.

Dr. Amen explains that "Your subconscious hears the words you say and takes them seriously. It does not have a sense of humor." This means that when you casually mutter to yourself, "I'm so stupid" or "I'll never get this right," your brain does not dismiss those words as a joke. Instead, it absorbs them as truth and begins to scan for evidence to confirm them. Over time, this process can become a destructive cycle where your own self-talk limits your success potential and shapes your daily behavior in damaging ways.

Dr. Amen uses the term "Automatic Negative Thoughts" to describe these habitual patterns of self-defeating language. One of the most dangerous forms of ANTs is called labeling. Labeling happens when you attach a negative identity to yourself or others. When you call yourself "lazy," "stupid," or "a failure," you are not just describing a moment of struggle; you are assigning yourself to a category and sealing in a judgment. Once the label sticks, your brain reinforces it by pulling up memories and associations that make it feel true. This is why labels are so dangerous. They become self-fulfilling prophecies.

To illustrate the seriousness of this problem, Dr. Amen has shared a story from his own family. His wife, Tana, once overheard their young daughter standing in front of a mirror, saying to her reflection, "I hate you. You are so stupid."

For a parent, hearing those words was devastating. Yet it also revealed something profound. The only thing worse than speaking cruel words to another person is speaking cruel words to yourself. Negative self-talk attacks from the inside, and it can be even more corrosive than external criticism.

The hopeful message in Dr. Amen's work, and our firm belief, is that this cycle can be broken. Just as harmful words can rewire your brain in negative ways, constructive words can help heal and strengthen it. Replacing ANTs with healthier patterns of thought is not about repeating shallow slogans. It is about speaking with accuracy and kindness, and in doing so, training your brain to create new, positive connections. When you shift the way you talk to yourself, you change the way you see yourself and, in turn, the way you act.

For this reason, your Never Say It list must include the language of labeling and self-condemnation. Never tell yourself that you are "worthless," "lazy," or "a failure." Never say that you will "never" succeed or that you "always" get it wrong. Never speak to yourself in words that you would not allow yourself to speak to a child you love.

Instead, follow Dr. Amen's prescription and replace those words with more truthful and constructive alternatives. Say, "That was a mistake, but I can learn from it." Say, "This is difficult, but I am capable of improving." Say, "I am growing stronger through this challenge." By changing the story you tell yourself, you change both the way your brain works and the direction of your life.

The words you choose do not simply describe your reality. They actively shape it. Guard your language carefully, especially the words you speak to yourself, because what you say to yourself, you eventually become.

Never Say It: Say This Instead

1. Labeling

- Never Say It: "I'm so stupid."
- Say This Instead: "That was a mistake, but I can learn from it."

2. All-or-Nothing Thinking

- Never Say It: "I always mess this up."
- Say This Instead: "Sometimes I struggle with this, but I am improving."

3. Fortune-Telling

- Never Say It: "I'll never succeed at this."
- Say This Instead: "I don't know how this will turn out yet, but I will give my best effort."

4. Mind Reading

- Never Say It: "Everyone thinks I'm a failure."
- Say This Instead: "I don't actually know what others are thinking, and I'm working on getting better."

5. Overgeneralization

- Never Say It: "Nothing ever works out for me."
- Say This Instead: "This didn't work out the way I hoped, but I've had other successes, and I can try again."

6. Discounting the Positive

- Never Say It: "That win doesn't really count."
- Say This Instead: "That was a real accomplishment, and I should give myself credit for it."

7. "Should" Statements

- Never Say It: "I should never make mistakes."

- Say This Instead: "It's normal to make mistakes. Each one teaches me something valuable."

8. Catastrophizing

- Never Say It: "If this goes wrong, it will be a total disaster."
- Say This Instead: "If this doesn't go perfectly, I can handle it and adjust."

Each of these categories represents a type of ANT that Dr. Amen identifies. By spotting them and swapping in healthier language, you can begin retraining your brain. Over time, this practice helps replace destructive patterns with more truthful, constructive ones.

Reflection Questions:

- What patterns of speech have you been reinforcing in your brain? Do they create fear or resilience?
- Can you recall a moment when someone's words gave you confidence like an athlete preparing for a competition?
- How might the words you use with your family or workplace be shaping the culture in unseen ways?
- If your words were studied like those tweets in the Penn study, what would they predict about your health and outlook?

4

THE INNER CONVERSATION: THE SECRET ALL PERSONAL DEVELOPMENT LEADERS SHARE

If you study the great teachers of personal development, you will notice something remarkable: despite differences in style, audience, and methods, they all return to the same truth. The way you speak to yourself and hold inner conversations shapes the trajectory of your life. Whether through affirmations, mindfulness, visualization, or reflective questioning, these leaders emphasize that words are not neutral. They are forces that either empower or restrict, that nourish resilience or reinforce fear.

From Norman Vincent Peale's mid-20th-century teachings on positive thinking to Louise Hay's focus on affirmations and self-love to modern voices like Brené Brown, Tony Robbins, and Gabrielle Bernstein, the consistent message is that the internal dialogue you maintain sets the limits of your growth and the possibilities for your success. What you tell yourself repeatedly becomes the narrative of your life.

Let's explore this through the stories and teachings of personal development leaders like Brené Brown, Wayne Dyer, Carol Dweck, Iyanla Vanzant, and Tony Robbins.

Brené Brown

"Talk to yourself like someone you love."

Brené Brown, a research professor and expert on vulnerability and courage, teaches that internal dialogue shapes our ability to act bravely. She emphasizes that we cannot be brave if our inner voice is shaming.

Brown encourages people to pay attention to the critical words they tell themselves and to replace them with affirming, compassionate language. During her early research, she noticed that participants often used self-condemning words they would never say to a friend.

Recognizing this, she developed exercises for shifting language from judgment to compassion. By practicing this daily, individuals began to approach challenges with courage instead of fear.

Wayne Dyer

"Change the way you look at things, and the things you look at change."

Wayne Dyer, a best-selling author and motivational speaker, urged people to "excuse-proof" their minds. He highlights how habitual self-criticism fosters patterns of failure, whereas deliberate, loving language can transform perception and behavior.

Dyer often told the story of a client who struggled with self-sabotage. By guiding the client to replace negative phrases like "I can't do this" with affirmations such as "I have the resources and skills to handle this," the client gradually developed confidence and achieved goals that had previously felt impossible. Ultimately, his teachings reveal that the words we internalize create a mental environment that either supports growth or stifles it.

Carol Dweck

"Becoming is better than being."

Carol Dweck, a psychologist and researcher best known for her work on growth mindset, shows the profound impact of internal dialogue on learning and achievement. Students who tell themselves "I am learning" rather than "I am failing" develop persistence, curiosity, and resilience.

In her studies, children who were encouraged to reframe mistakes as opportunities for growth not only improved academically but also reported higher motivation and engagement. This underscores that self-talk is not superficial; it directly influences how we interpret challenges, respond to setbacks, and pursue improvement.

Iyanla Vanzant

"Every time you speak to yourself with love, encouragement, and truth, you are reclaiming your power."

Iyanla Vanzant is a renowned motivational speaker, author, and life coach whose work has transformed the lives of thousands. She is best known for her books, *In the Meantime* and *Acts of Faith*, as well as her Emmy-winning show *Iyanla: Fix My Life*, where she helps people confront personal struggles and rebuild their lives through honest reflection and empowerment.

Vanzant's own life was marked by significant hardship. She grew up in a challenging environment, experiencing family turmoil and navigating early trauma. As a young adult, she faced the loss of her marriage and struggled with financial instability, all while raising her children. These experiences forced her to confront the power of her own internal dialogue and the importance of the words she spoke to herself.

Central to Vanzant's teachings is the power of self-talk. She emphasizes that the words we speak to ourselves are not merely thoughts. They actively shape our reality. In interviews and writings, she has said, "The way you speak to yourself creates your reality. If you tell yourself you are weak, unworthy, or incapable, that will be your experience. Speak life, speak power, speak possibility."

Deliberately cultivating positive internal dialogue allowed Vanzant to navigate personal setbacks, rebuild her life, and eventually become a powerful advocate for others.

Tony Robbins

"The words you attach to your experience become your experience."

Tony Robbins, a world-renowned life coach and motivational speaker, emphasizes "transformational vocabulary" as a cornerstone of personal growth. He explains that the language we use to describe experiences dictates our emotions and reactions.

Robbins often recounts stories of clients who reframed fear-based thinking, shifting from statements like "I am stuck" to "I am learning to overcome this challenge." This simple linguistic adjustment produces measurable changes in behavior and outcomes. By consciously choosing empowering words, we can shift from paralysis to action, from fear to confidence.

Ben Newman

"The conversations you have with yourself every day will determine the actions you take and the life you ultimately live."

Of course, we've already spoken about Ben Newman. Notably, Newman served as the mental conditioning coach for

Nick Saban's Alabama Crimson Tide, helping players develop the resilience, focus, and confidence required for elite competition.

Years before he ever joined the program, Newman was already cultivating the mindset that would lead him there. He practiced a daily affirmation: "I am the mental performance coach for Alabama football."

This wasn't just a motivational phrase. It was a deliberate act of self-talk and visualization.

At the time, Newman had no connections within the program. But by repeating his affirmation each day, Newman reinforced his belief in his capability and began aligning his actions, decisions, and efforts toward that future goal.

Newman's path to Alabama football reflects a core principle he teaches: the words we speak to ourselves are powerful tools for shaping reality. By focusing on what he wanted to achieve, rather than limitations or setbacks, he prepared himself mentally and emotionally to step into the role when the opportunity arose. By speaking life into his goals and committing to a mindset of success, he became an example of how belief in oneself can open doors to extraordinary and life-changing opportunities.

Byron Katie

"Don't believe everything you think."

Byron Katie, founder of The Work, a method of self-inquiry, shows that questioning and transforming painful thoughts is a direct route to freedom. She teaches that most suffering arises not from circumstances, but from the stories we tell ourselves about those circumstances.

Byron often shares stories of people trapped by thoughts such as *I am unworthy* or *I can't forgive*. Through her method of asking guided questions, individuals discover that the statements they assumed were true were in fact interpretations, not reality. Her approach illuminates how self-talk either ensnares or liberates us.

Eckhart Tolle

"Rather than being your thoughts and emotions, be the awareness behind them."

Eckhart Tolle, spiritual teacher and author of *The Power of Now,* highlights the autopilot nature of our internal voice. Negative self-talk, he explains, is often unconscious, yet it shapes emotions, perceptions, and behaviors. He recounts individuals who were unaware of their relentless inner criticism until observing it in meditation.

By learning to notice the thought patterns without attachment, they gained the freedom to redirect their mental energy.

Observing the inner dialogue and returning to presence transforms these mental patterns from traps into opportunities for clarity and peace.

Mel Robbins

"You are one decision away from a completely different life."

Mel Robbins, motivational speaker and author, offers practical tools like the 5 Second Rule to interrupt negative self-talk before it spirals. She teaches that small, deliberate actions can shift the tone of our internal dialogue, reinforcing confidence, courage, and self-encouragement.

In her workshops, she shares stories of clients who took five-second actions, such as sending a difficult email, starting a workout, or making a key phone call, that disrupted fear-laden internal chatter and created momentum toward success.

Don Miguel Ruiz

"Be impeccable with your word. Speak with integrity. Say only what you mean."

Don Miguel Ruiz, author of *The Four Agreements*, emphasizes that the words we use with ourselves and others act like seeds; positive language cultivates growth, while negative language undermines it. He shares examples from personal stories where small shifts in self-directed language led to profound changes in self-esteem, relationships, and clarity of purpose.

Deepak Chopra

"What you pay attention to grows. Speak to yourself with awareness."

Deepak Chopra, a physician and author blending Eastern philosophy with modern psychology, teaches that words carry energy that shapes consciousness and neurological pathways. Internal dialogue can either amplify stress or foster resilience. He shares studies on meditation and mantra use, demonstrating that when people speak or think positive, intentional phrases, cortisol levels drop, and cognitive function improves.

By speaking to ourselves with awareness and care, we actively influence our capacity for clarity, creativity, and emotional balance.

Gabrielle Bernstein

"The way you speak to yourself sets the tone for your entire life."

Gabrielle Bernstein, a spiritual teacher and motivational speaker, continues the teachings of Louise Hay, showing how affirmations and conscious self-talk reprogram limiting beliefs. She emphasizes that replacing inner criticism with self-support not only improves mental health but also enhances our ability to pursue purpose and joy.

Brendon Burchard

"Your internal dialogue either energizes or depletes you. Choose your words carefully."

Brendon Burchard, a high-performance coach and author, underscores that self-talk governs motivation, focus, and energy. Negative internal dialogue depletes us, whereas constructive, empowering statements enhance engagement and perseverance.

Burchard recounts clients who struggled with procrastination and self-doubt, who transformed their outcomes by scripting empowering internal statements each morning, reinforcing a growth-focused mindset.

Robin Sharma

"The mind is a garden. Your words are the seeds. Speak greatness into yourself daily."

Robin Sharma, author of *The Monk Who Sold His Ferrari*, connects mastery of self-talk to personal leadership and excellence. He compares negative self-talk to a silent enemy that erodes creativity, confidence, and determination, while deliberate, positive self-talk cultivates resilience, focus, and growth.

Sharma shares examples from leadership programs where participants rewired their internal narratives, leading to measurable improvements in productivity, decision-making, and emotional intelligence.

Esther Hicks

"Your thoughts create your reality. Speak to yourself in ways that uplift."

Esther Hicks, spiritual teacher of Abraham-Hicks, teaches that thoughts and words align us with the reality we attract. Fear-based or critical internal dialogue blocks our potential, whereas affirming, uplifting language enhances clarity, well-being, and personal manifestation.

Gabby Reece

"How you speak to yourself determines how you show up in the world."

Gabby Reece, a professional athlete, wellness advocate, and motivational speaker, highlights how internal language shapes performance, recovery, and resilience. She emphasizes that self-talk determines how we show up in all areas of life, from training to personal relationships to professional challenges.

Brian Cain

"Your self-talk is the foundation of your mental game. Speak to yourself like a champion."

Brian Cain is an international best-selling author and one of the world's foremost authorities on mental performance. He is the creator of The Mental Performance Mastery Coaching Certification Course and The 30 Days to Mental Performance Mastery for Athletes Program. He has worked with athletes and teams across the UFC, NBA, NFL, MLB, NHL, PGA, and NCAA, helping them develop elite mindsets and routines.

In his podcast, *Mental Performance Daily,* Cain emphasizes the importance of self-talk in achieving peak performance. He teaches that the words we use with ourselves shape our mindset and influence our actions. By cultivating positive and empowering self-talk, we can overcome obstacles and perform at our best when it matters most.

Tony Gaskins Jr.

"You can't win in life if you're losing in your mind."

Tony Gaskins Jr. is the acclaimed life coach, author, and motivational speaker who pulls no punches. He's the friend who tells you what you need to hear, not just what you want to hear, constantly focusing on the accountability required to build a great life rooted in self-respect. Tony often reminds people that you can't build a beautiful life on a shaky foundation. In his view, the shakiest foundation of all is a mind at war with itself. He argues that your success or failure begins in the trenches of your mind. His message is simple: if your self-talk is critical, doubt-ridden, and focused on past mistakes, you're already fighting an uphill battle. To win out there, you have to start winning in here by feeding your mind positive, powerful dialogue.

Brian Tracy

"Ninety-five percent of your emotions are determined by the way that you talk to yourself."

For decades, Brian Tracy has reigned as the seasoned CEO of self-improvement. His work isn't based on theory; it's based on the measurable actions that lead to results.

Based on his years of observing successful people, Brian emphasizes the sheer, overwhelming power of this internal loop on our feelings. It's about functionality. If your internal dialogue fuels anxiety, stress, or self-doubt, it negatively colors nearly all of your daily emotional landscape. His insights prove that changing your mindset isn't superficial; it's the most direct path to taking decisive control of your emotional state.

Lucinda Bassett

"What you say to yourself every day will either lift you up or tear you down."

Lucinda Bassett is a respected author, speaker, and mental health advocate who has dedicated her career to guiding others through the dark tunnels of anxiety and panic. She speaks with authority because she's been there, having battled a debilitating panic disorder herself. Her work is deeply compassionate and practical, focusing on the tactical steps needed to build mental strength and resilience.

Lucinda understands that the anxious mind is highly suggestible, listening intently to whatever you tell it. Her essential instruction for anyone struggling with negative thought patterns is to replace them with positive thoughts. By intentionally choosing thoughts of strength and hope over fear and worry, you are giving your mind a new, healthy script to work from and, in the process, reprogramming your life for peace and success.

Nick Vujicic

"You may have a lot of reasons to give up, but you also have a lot of reasons to keep going. I tell myself every day: 'I am capable, I am enough, and I can do this.'"

Nick Vujicic was born in 1982 in Melbourne, Australia, without arms or legs, a rare condition called tetra-amelia syndrome. From the very beginning, he faced immense physical and emotional challenges. Everyday tasks that most people take for granted were monumental obstacles, and as a child, he endured bullying and social isolation that made him question his worth and place in the world.

Despite these hardships, Nick's parents instilled in him a belief in his value and potential, a foundation upon which he could build his self-belief. Over time, Nick developed his own internal dialogue to reinforce that encouragement, telling himself, "I choose to focus on what I can do, not on what I can't."

As Nick grew older, he realized that his mindset and internal dialogue could not only transform his own life but also inspire others. He began speaking publicly about his experiences, sharing how the words we tell ourselves, combined with the affirmation of trusted supporters, can empower us to persevere. In his talks and writings, he emphasizes the importance of both internal and external encouragement.

Today, Nick is a globally recognized motivational speaker, author, and advocate, having delivered thousands of talks in over sixty countries. He has inspired millions to reframe their own self-talk, embrace challenges, and see possibilities where others might see limitations.

These stories remind us that the words we speak to ourselves are the most powerful tools we have. And when those words are reinforced by supportive voices around us, they can help us not only survive adversity but also thrive in ways we never imagined.

Across decades, styles, and disciplines, the pattern is clear. Whether spiritual, psychological, or practical in focus, every personal development teacher instructs that self-talk shapes thought, emotion, behavior, and ultimately, life outcomes. Conscious attention to our internal language strengthens resilience, nurtures confidence, and unlocks potential.

Practical exercises abound. Mindfulness and meditation help observe thoughts without judgment. Journaling externalizes internal dialogue for reflection and transformation. Visualization, affirmations, and cognitive restructuring embed constructive self-talk into the brain's neural network. Small, consistent habits, like pausing to replace a critical thought with an empowering one, reinforce neural pathways that support growth.

The words we carry inside are not incidental. They are a force that can either limit or expand the life we live. Self-talk is the foundation of transformation. Each internal word carries influence, shapes identity, choice, and reality. Cultivating awareness, choosing words deliberately, and practicing self-compassion transform self-talk from a source of limitation into a tool of empowerment, resilience, and purpose.

In the classroom, in the office, in private reflection, or in moments of challenge, the inner conversation is always present. By guiding it consciously, we align our thoughts with our highest potential. We shape who we are, how we act, and the life we create.

5

PUTTING THE SCIENCE INTO ACTION

Words do more than *express* what we think; they can actually *shape* what we think. They steer attention, regulate emotion, and influence how the brain connects experience to action. Over the past several decades, researchers have moved beyond intuition to measure how the language we use with ourselves and others reshapes behavior and even rewires neural circuits.

When people dismiss self-talk or affirmations as empty motivation, science tells another story. Controlled experiments, randomized trials, and neuroimaging studies show that the words we choose can change physiology, focus, learning, and relationships.

In other words, language is not decoration. It is a mechanism of change.

One of the deepest veins of research concerns the deliberate use of self-talk to improve performance. In sport psychology, researchers sought to determine whether athletes who talk to themselves in specific, structured ways actually perform better. The results were clear: meta-analytic reviews of decades of studies indicated that self-talk interventions produce small to moderate improvements in task performance and that motivational and instructional self-talk show consistent benefits when trained and practiced.[7]

When athletes use short, specific phrases to cue technique, manage arousal, or bolster confidence, measurable gains in performance follow. These findings emerged across dozens of trials and survived statistical synthesis, which is why sport psychologists today routinely teach athletes how to design self-talk scripts for practice and competition.

But how does repeating a phrase inside your head translate into calmer nerves or steadier execution?

Neuroscience shows that when people direct words to themselves, measurable shifts occur in brain circuits governing emotion and cognitive control. Negative, self-critical thinking and compassionate or goal-directed self-talk produce distinct patterns of activation. Negative self-referential thinking lights up the brain's threat and rumination networks, including the amygdala and connected midline cortical structures that sustain worry.[8] In contrast, compassionate or goal-directed self-talk engages networks associated with regulation, problem-solving, and emotional balance.

The clinical literature makes this practical. Cognitive behavioral therapy, built on the idea that thoughts drive mood and action, repeatedly shows effectiveness across hundreds of trials for depression and anxiety. Systematic reviews and meta-analyses conclude that CBT reliably reduces symptoms and that its techniques, which explicitly target automatic negative thoughts and cognitive distortions, are central to that success. Cognitive restructuring,the active reframing of automatic negative statements into more accurate and helpful alternatives, is one of the core mechanisms that explains CBT's effectiveness.[9]

These brain patterns are not just theoretical; they show up in real, clinically meaningful ways. Persistent negative self-talk is a defining feature of depression and anxiety. Brain-imaging studies have found that people who dwell on self-criticism show higher activity in self-focused networks and less engagement in the brain's control systems when they try to move away from negative thoughts. That helps explain why rumination so often leads to low mood and slower recovery. On the other hand, therapies that teach people to change these thought patterns lead to both emotional relief and measurable improvements in brain function. In short, changing your language changes your thinking, and changing your thinking changes your brain.[8]

When people learn to notice an automatic "I always fail" thought and replace it with "I have failed sometimes, and I can learn from this one," their affect, behavior, and problem-solving change in measurable ways. Large meta-analyses and network reviews confirm CBT's status as an evidence-based approach for common emotional disorders, and they show that the treatment's power lies largely in changing internally generated language.

Related but distinct is a growing literature on self-compassion, which reframes self-talk away from self-criticism toward supportive, accepting language. Meta-analytic work by Kristin Neff and others has shown that cultivating self-compassion reduces self-judgment, lowers stress responses, encourages healthier behaviors, and improves mood.[10]

Studies on self-compassion training show clear benefits. People who practice it tend to feel less shame and anxiety and become more emotionally resilient. Larger reviews of many studies find the same pattern: less self-criticism and better coping, even in the face of illness or pain. The science points to two main reasons.

First, compassionate language helps calm the body's stress response.

Second, it breaks the isolating cycle of shame that harsh self-talk often fuels.

Altogether, this research challenges the old idea that being hard on yourself builds motivation. In reality, kind and realistic self-talk supports both stronger mental health and more effective action.

Another robust body of research explores self-affirmation, which asks people to reflect on core values or strengths before facing a threat or challenge. Trials and population studies show that brief self-affirmation exercises reduce defensiveness, improve learning outcomes in students under stereotype threat, and even enhance health behaviors when delivered carefully.[11]

Self-affirmation helps widen your sense of self, so individual setbacks or threats feel less overwhelming. That shift makes it easier to respond with perspective instead of shame or avoidance. Research shows that even small changes in how people talk to and about themselves can lead to real improvements in learning, relationships, and health. The effect may be subtle, but it's consistent, measurable, and practical in everyday life.

When the focus shifts from the inner voice to how we speak to others, the science remains instructive. Language that invites perspective, validates experience, and reduces blame produces better social outcomes. Experimental work on communication shows that people who receive validating language during conflict become less defensive, more cooperative, and more likely to seek solutions. In contrast, language that labels, shames, or catastrophizes tends to escalate conflict and reduce problem-solving.

Research on persuasion and relationship repair shows how much language shapes connection. The way we frame feedback and the tone we use can either open doors or close them. Self-affirmation research supports this idea: when we feel secure and affirmed internally, we are less likely to react defensively or lash out to protect fragile self-worth.

Language also affects the body. Studies show that self-compassionate and encouraging self-talk are linked to lower cortisol levels and better regulation of the nervous system, whereas chronic self-criticism and hostile interactions are tied to higher stress hormones and markers of inflammation. In other words, the words we use with ourselves and others do more than shape emotions; they influence physiology. Over time, these patterns can affect sleep, immunity, and even long-term health. Shifting toward kinder, more constructive language offers measurable psychological and physical benefits.

Of course, not every study finds large or uniform effects. Reviews of the research note that results vary depending on the quality of training and the consistency of practice. The biggest benefits come when self-talk, self-compassion, and affirmation exercises are personalized, repeated, and connected to a person's real values, not treated as one-time pep talks. Researchers also emphasize the need for stronger follow-up data and better control comparisons. These limitations do not weaken the core insights; they make them more precise. They remind practitioners that meaningful change comes from structure, repetition, and context.[12]

One of the most powerful findings in recent psychology isn't about motivational speeches or "believing in yourself." It's about what happens when people take a quiet moment to remind themselves who they are and what they value. A 2024 study led by Geoffrey Cohen and David Sherman pulled together 144 independent studies on self-affirmation and found something remarkable: these simple exercises reliably improved both academic performance and psychological well-being. The overall effect size isn't just statistically significant; it's meaningful in real life.[13]

Here's the key: self-affirmations work best when they're personally relevant and repeated. Writing once about something you value (say, your integrity, family, or determination) can give you a small emotional lift. But returning to those core values regularly reinforces your sense of identity, especially in moments of stress or self-doubt. That's when the science shows the biggest gains. The students in these studies weren't being told they were "amazing" or "limitless." They were asked to reflect on what really matters to them, and that quiet act of self-anchoring changed how they handled challenges.

It's easy to see why this matters far beyond the classroom.

When you're criticized at work, miss a big opportunity, or find yourself in conflict, your natural reaction might be to get defensive or withdraw. But grounding yourself in your values, literally reminding yourself, "I care about growth" or "I value honesty," protects your sense of self so you can stay open instead of shutting down. That's not pop psychology; that's what decades of controlled studies now show.

So, the takeaway? Don't treat self-affirmation as fluff. Treat it as practice, like brushing your teeth, but for your sense of self. The science is clear: people who do it regularly don't just feel better. They perform better, think more clearly under stress, and handle feedback without losing their footing.

Putting these threads together yields practical implications grounded in science.

First, conscious language change works. Whether the goal is to reduce performance anxiety, overcome depressive rumination, or improve social repair, experiments and trials show that targeted changes in self-talk and interpersonal phrasing produce measurable benefits.

Second, the most effective approaches are specific, repeated, and context-sensitive. Simple scripts that cue technique for athletes, brief self-affirmation exercises before stress, and structured self-compassion practice all outperform casual exhortations.

Third, cognitive techniques that teach people to notice, label, and reframe automatic negative thoughts are core therapeutic ingredients. Meta-analytic evidence places those techniques among the most effective for common emotional disorders.

Finally, because language engages brain systems for belief and self-reference, repeated practices can change neural pathways and bodily stress responses, producing durable benefits when they are maintained.

These conclusions are not abstractions. Controlled clinical trials, well-powered meta-analyses, and converging neuroscience point in the same direction. Athletes who learn brief, focused self-talk gain steadier performance. Patients in CBT who challenge automatic negative thoughts recover more quickly than those without such training. People who practice self-compassion show reduced stress physiology and improved well-being. Students who receive self-affirmation interventions are more likely to persist in the face of stereotype threat. People who speak to others with validation and curiosity create calmer, more cooperative interactions.

Across methods and domains, the science validates a simple, consequential proposition: how we talk to ourselves and how we talk to others matters, and changing that language is a feasible, evidence-based strategy for improving psychological, social, and even physical outcomes.

So, on a practical level, how do we incorporate science-backed practices into our lives? Research keeps showing that small, teachable habits can make a real difference in how we handle pressure and stress. A few that show up again and again in studies:

- Notice negative self-talk. Catch automatic negative phrases when they pop up.
- Label without judgment. Acknowledge them for what they are: just thoughts, not facts.
- Replace them with something believable. Choose realistic, encouraging alternatives instead of empty positivity.
- Ground yourself in your values. Before situations that tend to trigger defensiveness, take a moment to remind yourself what really matters to you.
- Respond to setbacks with compassion. Use short, kind phrases instead of launching into self-criticism.
- In conflict, validate and invite collaboration. Name feelings and intentions, and look for ways to work together.

Over time, repeating these small practices can actually change how your brain and body respond under pressure.

The science does not promise perfection, but it does promise leverage. It gives us a reliable way to tilt attention, physiology, and behavior toward outcomes we prefer. The experimental evidence, the meta-analyses, and the neuroimaging studies together show that the voice in your head and the tone you use with other people are more than private musings; they are interventions you can learn, practice, and deploy.

The words you avoid and the words you choose matter not only for how you feel in the moment but also for how you learn, perform, relate, and how your brain is organized over time.

6

THE BROADER CONTEXT OF WORDS

When we think about the power of words, it is easy to focus on our immediate circles: our families, our classrooms, and our closest friends. But words ripple out far beyond those places. They shape how we heal, how we succeed, and how we endure in moments of testing. They can carry life or death into boardrooms, hospital rooms, and locker rooms. Proverbs reminds us, *"The tongue can bring death or life; those who love to talk will reap the consequences"* (Proverbs 18:21, NLT).

Nowhere is that more true than in three areas of life where words have a lasting impact: health, success, and performance.

Health and Healing

Language plays a pivotal role in medicine, extending beyond mere communication to a tool that can profoundly influence a patient's health and recovery. The words doctors use can shape a patient's mindset, expectations, and physiological responses to treatment. This concept of the psychology of language in medicine underscores the power of positive communication in healthcare.

In one study, for instance, the authors found a correlation between the use of direct negative messages and an increase in patient anxiety.[14]

Dr. Bernie Siegel, renowned for his compassionate approach to medicine, emphasized the profound impact of self-perception and internal dialogue on healing. He believed that many patients' struggles stemmed from an inability to love themselves, often due to past experiences of being unloved during crucial periods of their lives.

In his groundbreaking work, *Love, Medicine & Miracles,* Siegel introduced the concept of "exceptional patients," individuals who actively engaged in their healing process by fostering a positive self-image and nurturing inner strength.

He observed that these patients often refused to be victims of their circumstances. Instead, they educated themselves about their conditions and became proactive participants in their care. He noted that such patients frequently demonstrated a "fighting spirit," which was associated with better long-term survival outcomes.[15] This fighting spirit was not simply about willpower; it was a mindset cultivated through conscious, positive engagement with their own thoughts and emotions.

Central to Siegel's philosophy was the idea that hope and self-empowerment are vital components of healing. He asserted, "Refusal to hope is nothing more than a decision to die," underscoring the importance of maintaining a hopeful, positive mindset. He encouraged patients to speak to themselves in ways that reinforced their strength, resilience, and capacity for recovery. Affirmations such as "I am capable of healing," "I love and accept myself," and "I am willing to fight for my life" became tools for mental and emotional empowerment. By guiding patients to use positive self-talk actively, he helped create a therapeutic environment where healing was not just a medical process but a collaborative journey between mind, body, and spirit.

But what about when your doctors offer no hope for recovery? Dotie Osteen, the co-founder of Lakewood Church and the mother of pastor Joel Osteen, spoke healing to herself and overcame the odds. Diagnosed with metastatic liver cancer in 1991 and given only a few weeks to live, she turned to her faith and positive affirmations as part of her healing journey.

Dotie's approach to healing was deeply rooted in her belief in the power of God's word and the importance of speaking life over her circumstances. She emphasized the necessity of positive self-talk, stating, "I can't act sick; I have to act well." This mindset was instrumental in her daily routine, as she continued with her normal activities and focused on envisioning herself as healed. She also made a conscious effort to forgive others, recognizing that harboring unforgiveness could hinder her healing process. She likened unforgiveness to poison in the body, underscoring the significance of emotional and spiritual well-being in physical health.

Dotie's healing journey was marked by specific, faith-based declarations she spoke over her life, which are chronicled in her book, *If My Heart Could Talk*, and often shared by Pastor Joel. She believed that words shape reality. She affirmed, "I'm not going to die; I'm going to live and declare the works of the Lord," actively rejecting thoughts of sickness and insisting, "I am not a victim of this disease… I am a victor in Christ."

She used this practice to redefine her identity, not as someone sick, but as someone strong and overcoming. She affirmed, "I can have what God says I can have, be what God says I can be, and do what God says I can do."

Dodie's approach was also practical. She made a decision to live as if she were already healed, which meant saying things like, "I am getting better and better every day," which shifted her attention from present symptoms to her desired future. She refused to speak negatively about her illness and instructed her family to do the same, creating a positive environment that she believed was just as essential as her own words.

Ultimately, Dodie's commitment to faith and positive self-talk, coupled with her refusal to accept the terminal diagnosis, led to a remarkable recovery. Within two years, her body was cancer-free. Her healing serves as a powerful testament to the power of faith, positive thinking, and the importance of addressing both spiritual and emotional health.

Professional Success

The way we talk about achievement often reveals what we truly believe about ourselves. Many people unconsciously speak from scarcity: "I'll never get ahead." "Opportunities like that aren't for people like me." These phrases build invisible walls that keep success at a distance.

The late comedian Joan Rivers, renowned for her wit and resilience, demonstrated the power of positive self-talk throughout her life and career. Faced with countless challenges and setbacks, she adopted an internal dialogue that reinforced perseverance and possibility. Rivers once said, "If I can't make it through one door, I'll go through another door… or I'll make a door. Something terrific will come, no matter how dark the present."

This shows how she consciously encouraged herself to keep moving forward, viewing obstacles not as endpoints but as opportunities to uncover new paths. Her mindset illustrates a crucial principle of self-talk: By speaking to ourselves in empowering and solution-focused ways, we can navigate uncertainty with confidence and creativity, turning adversity into opportunity.

Scripture gives us a similar charge: *"Let us hold tightly without wavering to the hope we affirm, for God can be trusted to keep His promise"* (Hebrews 10:23, NLT). When our words align with hope rather than despair, we declare our trust not just in ourselves, but in the God who provides.

Consider the story of J.K. Rowling. Long before becoming one of the world's most beloved authors, she was a single mother living on welfare while facing repeated rejection from publishers as she wrote the *Harry Potter* series. At a point when many would have given up, her self-talk became a lifeline. She reminded herself, "I will finish this story; I am a capable writer."

These affirmations helped her push through doubt and uncertainty, keeping her focused on finishing and submitting her manuscript. Early encouragement from an editor who recognized her talent further strengthened this belief, giving her the courage to persevere through countless obstacles.

"I will finish this story; I am a capable writer."

Look also at the high-stakes world of the C-Suite, in which words are currency. The best executives recognize that communication, whether internal self-talk or public speech, doesn't just transmit information; it shapes culture, trust, and even stock price.

For them, a positive mindset is a critical business strategy.

Everyone experiences doubt, but what sets them apart is how they respond to it: the way they speak to themselves and the words they permit others to speak over them.

At Microsoft, one executive realized early that the way he viewed himself would shape every decision he made. Satya Nadella describes in his book *Hit Refresh* that negative self-talk could have held him back, but he learned to reframe it early by reminding himself that he could grow, learn, and embrace challenges. That deliberate internal dialogue became the foundation for a leadership style defined by risk-taking, empathy, and persistence.

"The view you adopt for yourself profoundly affects the way you lead your life."
– Satya Nadella

For someone like Sara Blakely, who would become the founder of women's shapewear brand Spanx, the challenge was different but equally intense. She had no formal training in fashion or retail, only a dream and a stubborn willingness to try. Instead of letting her lack of experience be a barrier, she told herself again and again that it was an advantage. It gave her the freedom to think differently. And when a friend encouraged her belief in her prototype, her self-talk became a tool for action, pushing her forward with confidence.

"Don't be intimidated by what you don't know. That can be your greatest strength and ensure that you do things differently from everyone else."
– Sara Blakely

Even seasoned executives face moments of insecurity. A CEO of a major social media platform described the tension between imposter feelings and the need to act decisively. She combated the doubt with a clear internal script: "I have the skills. I am prepared. I can lead," and leaned on trusted colleagues who reinforced her confidence. Those combined voices, her own and theirs, gave her the courage to make bold decisions under scrutiny.

The same was true for a global automaker stepping into a top role. He admitted to himself that failure was possible, yet he repeated affirmations of preparedness and capability: "I've prepared. I can handle this. I will figure it out." Facing the immense responsibility of running an iconic company, that inner dialogue allowed him to transform anxiety into decisive action.

Other leaders, like those taking over founder-led companies, have described similar experiences. Impostor syndrome is real, but pairing self-reassurance with validation from mentors can turn initial fear into early wins, reinforcing both confidence and capability.

Entrepreneurs often face the most extreme stakes. One cofounder likens acting on audacious ideas to jumping out of an airplane, trusting that you'll catch a bird flying by. It is the combination of self-talk and external support that transforms risk into tangible outcomes.

Across industries and roles, a pattern emerges: leaders who thrive do not silence fear; they acknowledge it. They speak to themselves with courage, absorb empowering words from others, and use that dual reinforcement to take decisive action. The inner voice can be your harshest critic or your strongest ally.

These examples show how deliberate self-talk and the encouragement of others can turn hesitation into momentum, uncertainty into leadership, and doubt into lasting impact.

Let's look at a few more examples.

As the former chief operating officer of Facebook (now Meta) and the founder of LeanIn.Org, Sheryl Sandberg has shaped global conversations about ambition, resilience, and the challenges women face in professional life. But beyond her high-profile career, she is also a deeply insightful observer of the human mind, especially the ways we talk to ourselves.

Reflecting on our inner dialogue, she writes in her book, *Option B*: *"We would never say [to a friend] … 'You know you're not attractive and you're boring.' Except a friend would never say that to her. She said it to herself. We would never say that to a friend, but we say that to ourselves."*

Sandberg's words cut to the heart of a common but destructive habit: the negative self-talk that quietly undermines confidence, limits ambition, and stifles growth. Her message is clear: resilience, performance, and well-being begin not only with external support but also with the inner kindness we extend to ourselves. By challenging this harsh inner critic and cultivating self-compassion, we can unlock our potential and sustain the confidence needed to navigate both personal and professional challenges.

One of the most relatable ways to understand negative self-talk comes from media executive and author Arianna Huffington. Best known as the co-founder of *The Huffington Post,* she is not only a major figure in business but also a leading advocate for wellness and reforming modern work culture.

After experiencing severe burnout in 2007, she shifted her focus from achievement alone to a broader idea of well-being, or what she calls the "Third Metric of Success." She later founded Thrive Global to challenge the collective belief that burnout is the price of success.

It is from this highly successful and deeply reflective vantage point that Huffington speaks about the constant barrage of internal criticism. She gives the inner critic a name that immediately resonates with anyone who has dealt with unwanted self-doubt: "the obnoxious roommate."

This "roommate," as Huffington describes it, is the perpetually negative, self-judgmental voice that "always puts me down, telling me I'm not good enough." It is the commentary track that fuels self-doubt and whispers warnings of failure, constantly attempting to undermine our actions and reinforce our deepest insecurities.

The brilliance of this analogy lies in its simplicity. You wouldn't tolerate a demanding, perpetually critical roommate in your home, yet we often allow this destructive inner voice to run unchecked in our minds. By naming and externalizing the voice, Huffington offers a crucial first step for anyone seeking to rewire their self-talk: recognizing that you are not the voice but the observer of it. Her message underscores that to succeed on your own terms, you must learn to "evict" or, at least, manage the obnoxious roommate through structure, repetition, and a conscious dose of wisdom.

Huffington's analogy sets the stage for understanding how shifting our internal narrative can transform not only our personal well-being but also how we lead and influence others. This connection becomes even clearer in the work of Jackie Insinger.

Jackie Insinger is a bestselling author, keynote speaker, and the founder of Spark Brilliance, a leadership development firm that integrates neuroscience and positive psychology to enhance team dynamics and performance. With degrees from Duke University and Harvard University, along with a certification from the MIT Sloan School of Management, she combines scientific research with practical strategies to help leaders foster authentic connections and drive organizational success.

In her work, Insinger emphasizes the profound impact of a leader's internal dialogue and outward communication on team morale and performance. She notes that a leader's mood and behavior are contagious; those who maintain a positive mindset and communicate with clarity and empathy create an environment where teams feel motivated and engaged.

Insinger also advocates for the "Platinum Rule," treating others the way they wish to be treated. She believes that understanding and respecting individual preferences fosters trust and collaboration within teams. She stresses the importance of psychological safety in the workplace, where team members feel free to express themselves without fear of judgment. Such environments encourage openness and innovation, leading to higher performance and engagement.

Through her research and methodologies, Insinger demonstrates that positive self-talk and intentional, empathetic communication are not merely soft skills but essential components of effective leadership, and leaders who cultivate these practices can help create supportive, resilient, and high-performing organizational cultures.

"As the leader, the power of your disposition is just as strong as the power of your position."
– Jackie Insinger

This philosophy was also the bedrock for Sam Walton, the visionary founder of Walmart and Sam's Club. He built his empire on a relentless, optimistic belief in his employees, recognizing that the only way to achieve his audacious goals was to empower every person to believe they could contribute. He made this principle a central tenet of leadership:

"Outstanding leaders go out of their way to boost the self-esteem of their personnel. If people believe in themselves, it's amazing what they can accomplish."

Whether you are leading a team of thousands or just the team of one that is your own life, the lesson is clear: your biggest opponent is not outside the door but behind your eyes. What will you tell yourself, and those around you, today?

The stakes in public life are the highest of all: words spoken by political leaders are not just opinions; they become the shared reality and guiding narrative for millions. The most transformative figures understand that true power lies in their ability to shape the collective mind, instilling courage, resilience, and hope when they are most needed.

The Engine of Belief

A century ago, President Theodore Roosevelt, a champion of ambition, action, and perseverance, centered the power of the mind in his philosophy. Roosevelt believed that inaction was the greatest enemy of progress, and the single biggest hurdle to taking action was the internal decision to limit oneself. He knew that confidence is the necessary first step on any challenging journey; if you allow doubt to creep in, your motivation stalls before you've even started. For him, belief was the ignition switch for achievement:

"Believe you can, and you're halfway there."

This simple directive is a rallying cry for self-belief, instructing the individual to silence the internal voice of limitation and recognize that the conscious choice to believe in success carries immense weight.

The Defiance of Optimism

This principle of mindset was tested on a global scale by Prime Minister Winston Churchill. During World War II, when the United Kingdom stood nearly alone against the overwhelming might of Nazi Germany, Churchill faced a nation consumed by doubt. His job was not to deny the danger but to frame a devastating reality in a way that unlocked the country's latent fighting spirit. He used his voice to combat internal and external fear, distilling the concept of positive mental attitude into a strategic contrast:

"A pessimist sees the difficulty in every opportunity; an optimist sees the opportunity in every difficulty."

Churchill's leadership was defined by his refusal to allow pessimism to become the national narrative. He used language to highlight opportunity and survival, making the choice to speak optimistically a national act of war that rallied a free people.

For these leaders, hope is not passive wishful thinking; it is the ultimate, active engine for change. By choosing to speak and act from a position of possibility, they showed that people can transcend limitations.

Even the most celebrated performers have wrestled with doubt. Viola Davis, one of the most acclaimed actresses of her generation, has spoken openly about the internal dialogue she maintained to keep going in a highly competitive and often judgmental industry. Growing up in poverty and facing systemic barriers in Hollywood, Davis frequently questioned whether she belonged on stage or screen.

She credits deliberate self-talk as a lifeline during those moments. Before auditions or high-pressure performances, she would tell herself, "I belong here. I am enough" as a way to quiet the negative voice that questioned her talent or place in the industry and to step confidently into each role.

Equally important was the encouragement she received from mentors, teachers, and colleagues early in her career. Hearing others recognize her talent reinforced the self-belief she was cultivating. That combination of internal and external reinforcement allowed her to persist through rejection, seize opportunities, and ultimately achieve acclaim, including an Academy Award and multiple Tony Awards.

"I belong here. I am enough."
– Viola Davis

Davis's journey illustrates a universal principle: the words we speak to ourselves and the ones we accept from those who believe in us have the power to shape our paths. Even in fields as subjective and challenging as acting, cultivating affirming self-talk and embracing supportive feedback can transform doubt into courage, hesitation into action, and potential into achievement.

Performance

Athletes understand the weight of words in a way few others do. One moment of discouragement can shake confidence; one phrase of belief can unlock a new level of performance.

Consider the story of Anthony Robles, a three-time NCAA All-American and 2011 National Champion wrestler for Arizona State University; his is a powerful example of how positive self-talk and a strong mindset can lead to extraordinary success. Born without a right leg, he faced significant challenges and skepticism throughout his athletic career. However, he credits his unwavering belief in himself, instilled by his mother, as the key to overcoming adversity. He often speaks about how his mother taught him to believe he was the only one capable of defining his own potential and not to let a challenge become an excuse. This foundation of positive self-talk allowed him to reframe his disability not as a disadvantage, but as a unique strength.

This mindset was evident in Robles' approach to wrestling. Instead of focusing on what he lacked, he honed the physical gifts he had, such as his incredible upper-body strength, to create a dominant and unconventional wrestling style that focused on immediate, winnable positions within a match, rather than the ultimate outcome.

Robles often says, "You grind now, you shine later," a phrase that encapsulates his philosophy of focusing on the hard work and small steps that ultimately lead to big achievements.

Robles' journey from walk-on at Arizona State University to undefeated national champion illustrates the tangible results of his mental fortitude. He had to overcome not only the physical demands of the sport but also the mental burden of proving himself to coaches, opponents, and himself. In interviews, he has shared how he learned to shift his mindset from being "good enough" to being "the best," a critical change that propelled him to the highest level of collegiate wrestling, and his story, chronicled in his autobiography *Unstoppable*, serves as a testament to the power of perseverance and the profound impact of believing in your own potential.

Novak Djokovic is another case study in the power of self-talk. He doesn't see mental strength as a gift; it's a skill he has deliberately trained, as he told fans on Tennis Warehouse, "No. Stop. I will have to correct you! My mental strength is NOT a gift. It is only something that comes with hard work!"

During matches, Djokovic uses self-talk to manage pressure and reset his mindset. One notable moment came in a 2022

Wimbledon quarterfinal against Jannik Sinner. Facing a two-set deficit, Djokovic took a break and repeated a mantra from Frank Herbert's *Dune*: "I will face my fear. I will permit it to pass over me and through me. And when it has gone past, I will turn the inner eye to see its path."

Even at the top of his career, Djokovic acknowledges the presence of self-doubt. In a conversation with Jay Shetty, he explained, "Every challenge, setback, and victory is an opportunity to reflect, strengthen your resilience, and tap into the strength you already have."

Djokovic's example shows how self-talk isn't just pep talk; it's a structured mental tool. When used intentionally, it can transform fear, fatigue, and doubt into focus, confidence, and performance.

We can also look at Misty Copeland's journey to becoming the first African-American principal dancer at American Ballet Theatre, defined as much by her internal dialogue as by her talent. Copeland faced systemic barriers in the classical ballet world and often confronted moments of self-doubt, wondering whether she truly belonged in an industry that had long overlooked dancers like her.

But through deliberate self-talk, Copeland continually reminded herself, "I am enough. I belong here," which became her anchor during grueling rehearsals, auditions, and performances, helping her silence the voices of doubt and criticism.

"I am enough. I belong here."
– Misty Copeland

Encouragement from mentors and teachers further reinforced her confidence. In interviews, she credits instructors who recognized her unique potential and repeatedly told her she could achieve greatness.

Like the ones that came before, Copeland's story demonstrates how the words we speak to ourselves and the ones we accept from trusted mentors can empower us to overcome systemic challenges, achieve unprecedented success, and redefine what is possible.

This is how language shapes success. We don't just build careers or businesses on strategies and spreadsheets; we build them on stories we tell ourselves.

Is money "something that always slips through my fingers" or "a resource I can learn to manage well"?

Is failure "proof that I wasn't cut out for this" or "evidence that I'm stretching beyond my comfort zone"?

One way of speaking narrows; the other opens it.

In each of these broader contexts, including health, success, and performance, the same truth emerges: words shape our reality. They are not lightweight. They can accelerate healing or hinder it. They can open doors to opportunity or slam them shut. They can unlock a champion or silence one before they begin.

Jesus Himself said, *"I tell you the truth, you can say to this mountain, 'May you be lifted up and thrown into the sea,' and it will happen. But you must really believe it will happen and have no doubt in your heart"* (Mark 11:23, NLT).

The mountains in our lives may look like illness, poverty, or fear of failure, but the words we speak to those mountains are not just sounds; they are declarations of faith, belief, and authority.

The broader context of words reminds us that no arena of life is exempt from their power. Whether on the hospital bed, in the boardroom, or under the stadium lights, our words will either breathe life or choke it out. The choice is ours every time we open our mouths.

Reflection Questions:

- Think about the words you speak about your own body or health. Do you often say things like, "I'm always injured," or "I'll never get better"? How might you replace those with life-giving phrases that affirm strength and resilience? Write down two new declarations you can begin speaking over your health this week.

- Reflect on the phrases you've caught yourself saying about money or your career. Have you been speaking about scarcity or abundance? Hopelessness or hope? What would it look like to declare words of faith and possibility over your finances and goals? Consider crafting one affirmation you can repeat daily.
- If you're an athlete, leader, or mentor, recall the words you've spoken to yourself or to others under pressure. Were they building up or tearing down? What phrase of encouragement can you begin using as a mantra in moments of stress or challenge?
- Read Proverbs 16:24 (NLT): *"Kind words are like honey… sweet to the soul and healthy for the body."* In what areas of your life do you need to pour "honey" rather than bitterness? How could that shift impact your relationships, your work, or your outlook?
- Write a short prayer or declaration committing to use your words as instruments of life in one specific area this week, whether that's your health, your career, or your performance under pressure.

7

THE NEVER SAY IT AGAIN LIST: ELIMINATE THESE PHRASES, CHANGE YOUR LIFE

Now that you have a better understanding of the power of words, we can begin to apply it more practically. As we've been discussing, words create your internal reality before they shape your external one. Often, we sabotage our future not through wrongdoing or direct destruction, but through subtle, habitual speech we've never stopped to question. We call this the "Never Say It Again List."

These everyday phrases carry hidden power to hold you back, reinforce limitations, and plant seeds of discouragement. You may not intend them negatively, but your brain doesn't know the difference. The goal of this chapter isn't just to identify these phrases but to reprogram your vocabulary with words that unlock growth, healing, and forward movement.

We're starting with ten, but once you begin paying attention, you'll be surprised by how many more you'll recognize in your daily language.

The Never Say It Again List

1. "I'm tired."

Why it's toxic:

Repeatedly declaring "I'm tired" doesn't relieve exhaustion; it actually reinforces it. Your brain listens, and your body complies. The phrase becomes a cue to slump, disengage, and underperform. It also sends subtle negative messages to anyone who hears you say it. Science shows that the more we reinforce fatigue with language, the more we disrupt the balance of cortisol and dopamine, worsening the sensation of tiredness.

Say instead:

- "I'm recharging."
- "I'm ready for what matters."
- "My energy is rising."

Bonus:

Curate your music playlists. Songs like "It's Gonna Be a Good Day" by Forrest Frank or "Speak Life" by TobyMac can shift your emotional and physical state faster than caffeine.

2. "I can't."

Why it's toxic:

This phrase locks the door to possibility. It's not just about admitting a limitation; it's agreeing with it. Every time you say it, your belief system gets smaller and smaller. Saying "I can't" activates defeat pathways in your brain. However, saying "I can't yet" keeps the door of neuroplasticity open.

Say instead:

- "I can't *yet*."
- "I'm learning."
- "I haven't mastered it, but I will."

Bonus:

Try the "just the way I want it" trick. Say your negative phrase, then add "and that's just the way I want it" to expose its absurdity. For example: "I'm always broke, and that's just the way I want it." Notice how that jars your mind? That discomfort is where the breakthrough begins.

3. "I'm just not that lucky."

Why it's toxic:

This phrase shifts all responsibility away from preparation, skill, or faith, placing it solely on randomness. It creates a victim mentality and kills motivation.

Say instead:

- "I create opportunities every day."
- "I'm well-positioned for favor."
- "I've got what it takes to win."

4. "This is impossible."

Why it's toxic:

This subtle complaint attracts more negativity. When you frame everything bad as your "luck," you reinforce a personal curse mindset, and faith becomes crucial.

Reframe:

- "This is temporary."
- "What's meant for me is on the way."
- "This is setting me up for something greater."

Faith upgrade:

Romans 8:28: "In all things, God works for the good of those who love Him." Say that out loud instead.

. . .

5. "That's just the way I am."

Why it's toxic:

This mindset reflects fatalism disguised as self-awareness. It suggests that growth is off the table, and you're admitting defeat.

Reframe:

- "That's how I've been, but I'm growing."
- "I'm choosing a better version of myself."
- "I'm being refined every day."

6. "I'll try."

Why it's toxic:

While it may sound harmless, this is one of the weakest commitments you can make. It provides a built-in escape from effort, accountability, or risk.

Reframe:

- "I will."
- "I'm committed."
- "Let's go."

7. "I have no choice."

Why it's toxic:

This mindset strips you of power, suggesting you are at the mercy of your circumstances.

Reframe:

"This book is an invitation into 'more.' Mapping a landscape where the boundary of outer and inner is not clearly delineated but influenced and nourished, each by the other, David invites us into the concept of gardening as a spiritual practice whereby we tend and nourish our garden while the garden equally tends to us, our soul space in particular. In the book, David illustrates how gardening is the ultimate locus of communion between the human heart and the Divine. The act of gardening helps to cultivate our emotions whereby we recognize the ability of the outer space to facilitate the exploration of the inner space which leads the soul into a deeper experience of 'the more.' David deftly demonstrates how emotions animate the soul and how the manner in which we engage and garden these emotions is reflected in the choices and actions we make. The garden is revealed as a dynamic and relational space that allows us to contemplate core human questions and facilitates us in approaching them. This is a well-researched, clear and beautiful book that is a challenge to 'any attempt to make the human soul small.' Thomas Berry famously stated that 'to plant a seed is to activate one of the deepest mysteries of the universe' and in this book David leads us some way into understanding why. A wonderful resource for gardeners and spiritual seekers alike, expanding in beautiful ways the horizon and context of both."

—**Niamh Brennan**, Lecturer in Eco-cosmology, South East Technological University, Waterford

"How delightful for gardeners to learn that their gardens actually cultivate them! A horticulturalist before becoming an Anglican priest, David White shows how gardening is an embodied contemplative practice that encompasses not only nurture but also pruning and eradication. The tranquil hours that we spend working in our gardens, inviting nature to express her true self, activate that affinity with the earth that is ingrained in our being. Gardening has a profound effect on our emotions. As we aim for a better future for our garden, we ourselves grow towards a more wholesome prospect. Contemplative gardening enables the feelings of love that surface as we work to turn into gratitude and the sad feelings to generate compassion and empathy."

—**Margaret Daly-Denton**, School of Religion, Theology and Peace Studies, Trinity College, Dublin

"An exploration such as David's into our severed connection with the Earth is of vital importance to our survival. It is the only remaining truth that binds us all together, a fragile dependence upon a mother that is calling us back home before she finally closes the door on a society that she can no longer support."

—**Mary Reynolds**, author of *We Are the Ark: Returning Our Gardens to Their True Nature Through Acts of Restorative Kindness*

"The history of gardening goes back to at least the third millennium BC. Gardens across many cultures were often considered sacred spaces symbolizing hope, transformation, and our connection with the Divine. Gardening can be seen as an art that has yet to fulfil its true potential and is driven by a desire for 'something more.' David White explores how the garden is the gateway to this 'something more.' Through contemplative spiritual practices, he considers selected emotions such as love, sadness, gratitude, and joy and brings us on a soul-gardening journey. The emotional experiences in the garden incite wonder, excitement, and connection, nurturing the soul and leading us onward towards discerning what embodied spiritual practices may help with our journey ahead. At a time of global crisis, this book shows us how contemplative gardening can help us to see through to the heart of things, to see through to the reunion of humanity, nature and the Divine."

—**Bríd Kennedy**, author of *Spirituality of Flowers: What Flowers Do for Us*

- "This is hard, but I choose my response."
- "I'm responsible for my decisions."
- "I always have the next move."

Faith upgrade:

God never calls you to powerlessness. Free will is sacred, as is your voice.

8. "It's too late for me."

Why it's toxic:

This assumption suggests that time is against you and that your best years are behind you. The truth is that the graveyard is full of individuals who died with potential still within them, not because they ran out of time but because they believed this lie.

Reframe:

- "Now is the perfect time."
- "God's not done with me."
- "I'm just getting started."

9. "I'm not good enough."

Why it's toxic:

This phrase fuels imposter syndrome, crushes creativity, and directly contradicts how God sees you.

Reframe:

- "I am equipped for this."
- "God qualifies me."
- "I am growing into greatness."

Faith upgrade:

- Gideon was called a "mighty warrior" by God.
- Moses struggled with stuttering, but God gave him the words he needed.
- David was dismissed, yet God made him king.

10. "I don't feel like it."

Why it's toxic:

This phrase is the ultimate dream killer. Most of what is worth doing in life happens when you don't feel motivated. Athletes and entrepreneurs know this.

Reframe:

- "Discipline over emotion."
- "Standards over feelings."
- "I'm showing up anyway."
- "My feelings will follow my actions."

11. "It's his fault, not mine."

Why it's toxic:

Blame may feel good in the short term, but it gives your power away to someone else. If it's always someone else's fault, you can never fix it, and you lose all your agency.

Reframe:

- "I am responsible for how I respond."
- "I can't control others, but I can control my choices."
- "I own my outcomes."

These phrases don't just come out of your mouth; they come from your beliefs. Change your words, and you'll begin to see where your mindset needs healing. This is not about perfection; it's about progress with intention.

8

REPROGRAMMING YOUR SPEECH FOR SUCCESS

Hopefully, by this point, you understand the power of your words. You've recognized the negative language that tears down and have begun replacing it with words that build up. This chapter is designed to help you take the next step: practice. Awareness alone does not lead to transformation. Lasting change requires repetition, intention, and structure.

Your default speech patterns are not accidental. They are programmed, shaped by years of repetition from parents, teachers, friends, media, and your own inner dialogue. Unless you intentionally rewrite them, your mind will drift back to what is familiar, even if it is destructive.

The good news is that, as previous chapters demonstrate, both science and scripture affirm you can reprogram your words and your future. This chapter shows how these principles work together in practical, daily rhythms.

Here are five practical ways these truths come to life.

1. The Power of Daily Declarations

Words that are repeated consistently become beliefs. Beliefs drive behaviors, and behaviors create results. Therefore, if you want to change your results in your business, relationships, health, or leadership, you must start by changing your declarations.

Neuroscience calls this reinforcing positive neural pathways. Scripture calls it meditating on truth and speaking life:

- *"Let the weak say, 'I am strong'"* (Joel 3:10).
- *"Faith comes by hearing"* (Romans 10:17).

Modern achievers model this too. Steph Curry, Oprah Winfrey, and Muhammad Ali, long before the world believed them, their words shaped them into legends. But declarations are not reserved for icons alone. They work for students, parents, entrepreneurs, and leaders in every walk of life.

Examples of "I Am" Statements:

Personal Growth

- I am confident, calm, and centered today.
- I am disciplined; I do what needs to be done.
- I am focused and productive with my time.

Family and Relationships

- I am a source of encouragement to my spouse and children.
- I am patient, kind, and compassionate in my words.
- I am creating a legacy of love, faith, and integrity in my family.

Business and Career

- I am a creative problem-solver who brings value to every situation.
- I am a magnet for opportunities and the right connections.

- I am an excellent communicator and leader.

Health and Wellness

- I am strong, healthy, and full of energy.
- I am making choices today that fuel my long-term health.
- I am grateful for a body that serves me well.

Faith and Identity

- I am fearfully and wonderfully made in the image of God.
- I am equipped, anointed, and chosen for this season.
- God has gone before me; I walk in boldness, peace, and faith today.

Leadership and Influence

- I am a voice of clarity and wisdom in my organization.
- I am helping others rise by speaking life into them.

Tactic: Write down three to five "I Am" statements. Keep them present-tense, emotional, and anchored in truth. Speak them out loud every morning.

2. Reframing Negative Thoughts into Positive Declarations

Transformation is not only about what you start saying. It's also about what you stop saying. Every complaint, fear-filled phrase, or self-criticism is an instruction to your mind.

Here's how to flip them in real time:

Negative Thought	Reframed Declaration
I'm overwhelmed.	I'm equipped to handle what is in front of me.
This always happens to me.	This is temporary, and I'm learning from it.
I'm stuck.	I'm in transition; forward is still forward.
I'll probably mess this up.	I'm prepared; I'm ready; I've got this.

This mirrors what cognitive-behavioral therapy teaches: catch the thought, confront it, replace it.

Example: During the 2008 financial crisis, Starbucks was collapsing. Instead of saying, "We are failing," CEO Howard Schultz reframed it for his team: "We are returning to our core and rebuilding our future." Those words shifted the company's trajectory, and today Starbucks thrives.

Reframing Formula:

1. Notice the negative statement.
2. Say it out loud.
3. Follow with, "But the truth is…" and declare life instead.

3. Eliminating Negative Speech

You've spotted the big offenders like "I'm so stupid" and "I can't catch a break." But subtle phrases like "That's just my luck," "This is killing me," and "Nothing ever changes" can sabotage you too.

These are not harmless. They train your subconscious to expect defeat.

Detox Plan:

- Run a seven-day speech audit. Track your words in a journal or phone.
- Each night ask: *Did I complain, curse, or blame? Did I build, bless, and declare?*

Interrupt Negativity: When you slip, immediately say, "Cancel that. I take that back. The truth is… "

4. Curating Your Inputs

You cannot speak life consistently if you are constantly consuming negativity.

Social media, podcasts, music, and conversations all shape your speech. If your feed is filled with outrage, gossip, and comparison, you're programming your words for cynicism.

Action Steps:

- Unfollow accounts that trigger jealousy or fear.
- Block or mute sources of outrage and gossip.
- Replace these sources with voices that promote encouragement, wisdom, and faith.

Music Tip: Uplifting lyrics lower stress and improve resilience. Build a playlist that recharges your spirit (e.g., "Speak Life" by Toby Mac or "Confidence" by Sanctus Real).

5. Guarding Your Circle

Words are contagious. Surrounding yourself with complainers and critics will shape your own speech.

Scripture warns:

"Do not be misled: Bad company corrupts good character" (1 Corinthians 15:33).

Leaders know culture is shaped by conversation. Jeff Bezos, for example, cut off negative talk in Amazon meetings, redirecting focus to solutions. He knew unchecked negativity spreads like wildfire.

You can still love people without letting them poison your speech:

- Set boundaries with toxic influences.
- Redirect gossip toward gratitude.
- Spend more time with people who speak life.

If you want to elevate your life, elevate your conversations.

What you speak today shapes what you believe tomorrow. What you believe tomorrow shapes the person you'll become next year. Reprogramming your speech is not about perfection; it's about practice. And it begins with the next sentence you say.

Reflection Questions:

- What default phrases do you find yourself saying most often? What mindset do they reinforce?
- Which three declarations would most powerfully shift your perspective right now?
- Who in your life drains your speech with negativity? What boundaries could you set?
- How might changing your inputs (social, digital, conversational) affect your words?
- If you led your home, team, or company with life-giving words, what culture would form?

9

WORDS THAT SHAPE FAMILIES AND GENERATIONS

Some of the most powerful words ever spoken aren't found in history books or recorded on microphones before cheering crowds. They are whispered at kitchen tables, spoken in bedrooms at bedtime, or declared in the middle of ordinary days.

They are the words parents speak to their children. They are the words children grow up carrying like invisible scripts that guide their choices, shape their self-worth, and echo into their futures.

The Bible is clear about this:

"Train up a child in the way he should go, and when he is old he will not depart from it" (Proverbs 22:6).

Training isn't just about rules, chores, or discipline. It is about the way we speak to our children. The words they hear most often in their home will shape the way they see themselves and the way they interpret the world.

Nancy Edison and Thomas: The Power of Reframing

When young Thomas Edison brought home a sealed letter from school, he handed it to his mother, Nancy, and asked her to read it. As soon as Nancy scanned it, tears filled her eyes.

She read aloud to her son:

"Thomas, your teachers say you are too brilliant for them to teach. They don't have the resources to help someone as gifted as you. From now on, I will educate you at home."

Those words lit a fire in Thomas. He grew up believing he was brilliant, creative, and capable of doing things others could not.

What he didn't know until after Nancy died was that the letter had actually labeled him *mentally deficient* and unfit for school.

Yet by the time he discovered the truth, it no longer mattered. His mother's words had already shaped his belief, and his belief had already shaped history. Thomas Edison went on to hold more than one thousand patents, inventing the phonograph, the motion picture camera, and, of course, the light bulb.

That story forces us to ask: What kind of "letters" do our children carry into adulthood? Do they carry shame-filled words like weights around their necks? Or do they carry words of possibility that help them believe in the brilliance God has placed inside them?

Ben Newman: Two Voices, Two Legacies

It's hard to imagine a better example than the life of Ben Newman.

Today, Ben is a *USA Today* Top-5 mental performance coach, best-selling author, and speaker. But just days before his eighth birthday, he lost his mom to a rare and devastating illness, amyloidosis.

Though chronically ill, she fought fiercely. Every evening, battling weakness and tethered to an IV, she would still find her way to the dinner table, look Ben in the eyes, and ask him about his day at school.

Her presence and her voice became his first taste of unwavering love and affirmation. In her journal entries, she scrawled powerful words that became both a lasting legacy and an emotional beacon for Ben:

"Beat the statistics. Beat the odds. Live with the disease that is chronic and fatal. Believe in yourself. Combat anything. Purpose in life."

These were not just affirmations; they were the sparks of resilience that would fuel his entire life.

Still, the encouragement he received coexisted with deep pain. After his mom's death, Ben lived with his father, who struggled with addiction and mental illness. His once-loving home environment turned harsh; the words he endured were so wounding that he later reflected, "I wish my dad would have just punched me, because the bruises would have gone away."

Ben's story illustrates both sides of the parental speech coin:

1. Words of love and encouragement have the power to spark enduring strength. His mother's tender questions and purposeful journal entries gave him love, worth, and purpose.
2. Words of degradation and criticism leave scars that last lifetimes. His father's verbal abuse created wounds deeper than any physical blow.

The impact of a parent's words continues to resound in modern stories.

- Serena and Venus Williams's father, Richard, told his daughters, "You're going to be champions. You're going to change the game." Even when the world doubted them, his confidence became the lens through which they saw themselves.

- Tiger Woods's father, Earl, repeated, "You're chosen for greatness," creating a sense of destiny that fueled his discipline.
- Michael Jordan's father, James, often teased him as the least athletic of his siblings. Rather than crush him, those words sparked a fire that turned him into the fiercest competitor of his era.
- Steve Jobs's adoptive father, Paul Jobs, assured him, "We're going to make you feel special." That affirmation laid the foundation for resilience through rejection and innovation.
- LeBron James's mother, Gloria, declared, "You were born to shine." Those words carried him through instability and helped forge one of the most impactful careers in sports history.

Most of us don't set out to harm our children with words, but in moments of stress or exhaustion, careless phrases slip: "You're always messing things up." "Why can't you be more like your sister?" "You'll never learn."

We may forget those sentences as quickly as we speak them, but children rarely do. They take root.

The good news is, positive words take root, too. We know neuroscience confirms this: repeated affirmations literally rewire the brain, strengthening pathways of confidence and possibility.

This doesn't mean avoiding correction. Nancy Edison didn't tell Thomas he was already a genius. She told him he was capable of learning in ways others didn't understand. Life-giving words don't ignore problems; they place them inside a bigger story.

Practical Family Practices

- Adopt short statements to repeat together:

"We are children of God."
"We are kind."
"We are strong."
"We don't give up."
"We love one another."

- At dinner, go around and have each person affirm someone else.
- Slip notes into lunchboxes or backpacks: "You are brave. I believe in you."
- Swap "You never listen" with "Let's try again together."
- Before bed, place a hand on your child's shoulder and declare, "You are loved. You are chosen. God has a big purpose for your life."

Repeated night after night, these words echo into adulthood.

Even when we understand how deeply words shape us, many of us still struggle to speak well of ourselves. Cultural messages about humility, likability, and self-promotion can make empowerment feel awkward or wrong. Before we explore tools for speaking life, we must understand why using our voices confidently often feels so uncomfortable.

Reflection Questions:

- What sentence from your childhood, whether life-giving or destructive, still echoes in your memory?
- If your children or loved ones repeated the three

phrases they hear from you most, what would they be?

- Imagine it's twenty years from now. What do you hope your children say about the words you spoke into their lives?

10

WHEN SPEAKING HIGHLY OF YOURSELF FEELS WRONG

We live in a world that tells us to believe in ourselves but punishes us the moment we actually do.

For many people, especially women, there is a deep discomfort with saying anything that might sound self-promotional. The fear is not just about appearing arrogant. It is about belonging: not seeming "too full of yourself," not alienating others, and not violating the unwritten social rule that likability matters more than confidence.

Yet, language matters. If we cannot *speak* highly of ourselves, it becomes nearly impossible to *think* highly of ourselves for long.

The Problem: When Humility Turns Into Self-Erosion

False humility can wear a mask of virtue. We downplay accomplishments, soften our strengths, and preemptively make jokes to disarm any hint of pride: "I just got lucky." "It is not a big deal." "Anyone could have done it."

We do this because it feels safer and because we learned, often from an early age, that confidence can make people uncomfortable.

Research supports this. Psychologists Victoria Brescoll and Eric Uhlmann found that women who self-promoted in workplace settings were often judged as less likable and less hireable than men making the same statements. The "double bind" is real: be confident, but not too confident; be proud, but in a way that reassures others you are still humble.

From childhood, many girls are taught to make themselves smaller in conversation. Compliments are deflected: "Oh, this old thing?" Achievements are downplayed: "It was not just me." Success is explained away: "I was in the right place at the right time."

Men are affected too, but in a different way. They are often expected to project confidence at all times, which can lead to overcompensation or a struggle to separate genuine pride from ego.

With both women and men, though, the outcome is the same. We develop a distorted relationship with self-acknowledgment. We either avoid it altogether or express it in ways that feel performative and hollow.

One person I coached told me, "If I sound too confident, I lose people. If I sound too modest, I lose myself."

That tension is one many of us live with.

The Science: Why Your Brain Believes What You Say

Neuroscientific research on self-talk indicates that your brain encodes language about the self as identity cues. When you say "I'm terrible at this" or "I'm not that impressive," even jokingly, your brain treats that as data. It adjusts the self-schema, or the mental framework you use to understand who you are and what you can do.

Conversely, when you acknowledge your competence or progress out loud, you strengthen neural pathways that support confidence and resilience.

As we discussed earlier, the 2024 study by Geoffrey Cohen

and David Sherman found that people who engaged in short, structured exercises affirming their values and capabilities showed measurable improvements in both academic performance and emotional regulation. Language, in other words, has a measurable effect on how we perform, meaning when you repeatedly downplay your strengths, you are not merely being polite. You are training your brain to question your own legitimacy.

Let's revisit the story of Serena Williams from Chapter 3. After one of her Grand Slam wins, when asked how she managed to keep succeeding under pressure, she replied, "I'm Serena, and that's enough."

That statement is simple but radical. It is not arrogance. It is clarity. Williams was not comparing herself to anyone or exaggerating her abilities. She was simply acknowledging her worth.

If she had instead said, "Oh, I was lucky today," the message to her own mind and to everyone watching would have been entirely different. When you own your excellence, you give others permission to own theirs.

We can look to Michelle Obama as another example. Never raised with the same unearned confidence that many men take for granted, Michelle has spoken often about the discomfort many feel around confidence. During a podcast conversation, she remarked, "Women, as we age, we get pushed out of the picture." She added that for much of her life, she found herself qualifying her statements and apologizing because she did not feel she had the inherent right to be outspoken. She also has acknowledged ongoing self-doubt. At a school talk in London, she shared, "I still have a little [bit of] impostor syndrome. It never goes away."

Her journey illustrates what it takes to shift from shrinking to speaking with integrity. She reframed "self-promotion" not as boasting, but as self-representation. She came to see that by withholding her achievements, she was failing to fully serve others with her experience and voice.

The goal is not to become someone who constantly announces how great they are. It is to build a vocabulary of accurate self-acknowledgment, one that reflects truth, not ego.

Here are several strategies:

1. State Facts, Not Opinions

Instead of "I'm amazing at this," say, "I have built significant expertise in this area over the past few years." Facts carry confidence without arrogance.

2. Share Credit Without Erasing Yourself

You can say, "I'm proud of what our team achieved, and I'm especially proud of the strategy I led that helped us get there." You acknowledge collaboration and your individual contribution.

3. Replace Apologies with Appreciation

If you're tempted to minimize your success ("I know I'm talking about myself too much"), pivot to gratitude: "I'm grateful for the chance to do work I care about." It frames confidence as gratitude, not self-centeredness.

4. Practice Micro-Confidence

Begin small by acknowledging one daily win, even if only to yourself or in writing. "That meeting went well." "That idea had traction." Over time, your comfort level grows, and the statements feel less foreign.

5. Anchor It in Service

Confidence becomes off-putting only when it is self-serving. Frame your strengths around value: "I created a process that improves client outcomes by 20 percent." That centers on contribution instead of comparison.

6. Rehearse New Language

Write or say aloud a few "proud but grounded" statements about yourself, such as:

- "I'm proud of how far I've come in this journey."
- "I worked hard for that opportunity, and I'm glad it showed."

- "That project required serious effort, and I'm glad it had impact."

Confidence and humility are not opposites. The most authentic humility does not come from denying your strengths but from recognizing them as gifts you can use well.

When you speak truthfully about your abilities, without inflation or apology, you invite others to do the same.

The goal is not to brag. The goal is to be honest. And honesty, when it comes to your own worth, is the quietest and most radical form of confidence there is.

11

PRACTICAL APPLICATIONS: HOW TO SPEAK LIFE INSTEAD OF DESTRUCTION

You've seen the science, studied the scriptures, uncovered toxic phrases, and started replacing them with truth. Now it's time to apply this knowledge to your everyday world, focusing on the areas where your words matter most: your inner life, your family, and your workplace.

This chapter is about action. If your words can shape your world, you need to be intentional about the kind of world you're creating.

The three arenas where your words carry the most weight are in your own life, within your family, and within your workplace. Let's look at how to reprogram your speech in each area.

Within Your Life

The person you speak to the most is yourself. Research shows we have more than fifty thousand thoughts per day, and a large portion of them are repetitive. If you are not intentional, the inner voice that plays in your mind can default to criticism, fear, or limitation.

Examples of negative self-talk include:

- Saying, "I'm so behind," the moment you wake up.
- Calling yourself lazy when you forget something.
- Criticizing your appearance in the mirror.
- Rehearsing failure before a big presentation.

Instead, replace automatic insults with gentle accountability and faith-filled declarations.

The truth is that the way you speak when no one is listening determines how you show up when everyone is watching.

Instead of	Say
"I'm so stupid."	"I'm still learning and growing stronger."
"I'll probably mess this up."	"I'm prepared and giving my best."
"I hate the way I look."	"I'm grateful for my body, and I'm caring for it daily."
"I can't believe I did that again."	"That's not who I'm becoming. I am moving forward."

Athletes use this principle every day. Before a college football game, players often repeat short affirmations like, "We are ready, we are prepared, we are winners." If it works for world champions under the brightest lights, it can work for you in the daily battles of your own life.

Within Your Family

Your words create and heavily influence the atmosphere of your home.

What does destructive speech sound like in a family atmosphere?

- Sarcasm after long days.
- Passive-aggressive comments that cut deeper than they help.
- Withholding praise with the excuse, *"They should already know."*

What if instead, your home became a sanctuary of encouragement?

Speak Life Into	Sample Words
Your spouse →	"I see how hard you work. Thank you for showing up every day. I love you."
Your kids →	"I love you. You are kind, creative, and chosen for a purpose."
Your parents →	"I love you and appreciate everything you've done for our family."

Challenge:

- Speak one life-giving sentence to each person in your home daily for seven days.
- Eliminate sarcasm as humor and replace it with affirmations.

Words can create homes where children thrive, marriages heal, and parents feel honored.

Within Your Workplace

You do not need the title of CEO to be a leader. Every word you speak at work contributes to the culture, morale, and productivity of the team.

Examples of negative patterns include:

- Complaining during meetings.
- Gossiping about coworkers.
- Downplaying your ideas and minimizing your wins.

Instead, use words that foster solutions and build momentum.

Language to Eliminate	Replace With
"This place is a mess."	"Let's find a better system that works."
"I hate meetings."	"How could we make this time more meaningful?"
"That's above my pay grade."	"I'd love to learn how to contribute at that level."
"They never listen to me."	"I will speak up with clarity and courage."

In 2006, Ford was on the brink of collapse. Morale was low, billions were being lost, and competitors were outpacing them. Then Alan Mulally became CEO. In his first meetings, instead of tolerating the usual pessimism and blame, he introduced a new vocabulary: *One Ford, One Team, One Plan, One Goal.* He refused to let negativity dominate. Instead, he repeated phrases like, "We will succeed as one company," creating a unifying vision.

Within a few years, Ford became the only major U.S. automaker to avoid a government bailout during the financial crisis. Mulally's words helped turn despair into determination and determination into profit.

Faith at Work:

Scripture reminds us:

- *"Do everything without grumbling or arguing"* (Philippians 2:14).
- *"Let your conversation be always full of grace"* (Colossians 4:6).

Speaking words of life at work is one of the most practical forms of leadership you can bring to your team.

Challenge:

When facing difficulty, be it financial pressure, family crises, or disappointment, your words shape your mindset. Choose words like:

- "This is stretching me, but I'm growing."
- "God is with me in this valley."
- "I don't know the outcome, but I trust the process."

Ultimately, if you want to change your words, you need to measure them. Here are three strategies to try:

Strategy 1: Word Audit

Track your words for a week. Highlight recurring complaints and notice where you consistently build or break.

Strategy 2: Speak-Out-Loud Journaling

Each morning, record a sixty-second voice memo declaring your vision for the day. At night, reflect: *Did my words align with my values?*

Strategy 3: Accountability Partner

Find a friend or coworker who also wants to improve speech habits. Check in weekly with each other and ask:

- What toxic phrase did you eliminate?

- What life-giving affirmation replaced it?

Reflection Questions:

- When you wake up, what are your first thoughts? How could you reframe them for the better?
- What is one positive affirmation your family needs to hear from you this week?
- How does your language contribute to your workplace culture?
- What negative phrases do you need to eliminate immediately from your vocabulary?
- Who could serve as your accountability partner for your speech habits?

If you truly believed your words carry power, would you still speak the way you do?

Words are literally the steering wheel of your life. They direct your inner world, your home, and your workplace. Speak life into your future, your family, your faith, your career, and your health.

Your words ultimately become your destiny, so choose them wisely.

CONCLUSION + 30-DAY CHALLENGE

Every day, you are just one sentence away from a new story and potentially a different life. You've discovered that words are not merely tools. They are not casual, background noise, or meaningless.

Words are creative, directional, spiritual, chemical, and habit-forming. Your words are like seeds, and everything you've planted so far is either blooming or bearing thorns in your mindset, relationships, health, faith, or work. The best news is that you can start planting something new right now.

This is not just theory; it is truth backed by scripture, science, and experience. Scripture says, "Life and death are in the power of the tongue" (Proverbs 18:21). Science shows that your brain literally rewires based on the words you repeat. Through experience, we all recognize that we've been changed and either built up or torn down by something someone has said to us at one point or another.

Your challenge now is to choose to speak daily with positive intention. This is your invitation, not to be perfect, but to be purposeful. This thirty-day challenge will help you eliminate toxic or negative self-talk, reinforce positivity in your life, and help you become the person who builds instead of breaks with your words.

Week 1

- Track your speech daily.
- Journal any recurring phrases, especially negative ones.
- Choose one negative self-image phrase to eliminate.
- Replace it with a new declaration.
- Speak three life-giving statements out loud each morning.

Week 2

- Add a new daily declaration.
- Flip limiting language in real time.
- Clean up your social media feed and inputs.
- Invite a friend to join the challenge.

Week 3

- Speak one encouraging word daily to someone.
- Remove sarcasm and negativity from your conversations.
- Journal emotional and spiritual shifts.
- Add a scripture-based declaration to your morning routine.

Week 4

- Speak blessings over your future.
- Record one-minute voice memos affirming who you are becoming.
- Reflect on who you were thirty days ago and celebrate the change.

Post-Plan Review:

- Which NSI phrase was hardest to stop saying? Why?
- Which new declaration felt most powerful?
- How did your mindset, energy, and relationships shift?
- What will you speak over the next thirty days?

Lord, help me to use my words to uplift, encourage, and bring life. May my speech reflect your truth, love, and faith. Let me build others up and never tear them down. Help me to speak boldly when needed, gently when necessary, and always with grace. Transform my mind, train my tongue, and shape my future one word at a time. In Jesus' name, Amen.

Let this not be the end but the beginning of a shift in how you speak, how you believe, and how you live your life daily. Remember, you were created in the image of God, who spoke the universe into existence.

So speak with vision, speak with faith, and speak with life. Because what you say today shapes who you become tomorrow.

REFERENCES

1. Psych Central. 2019. "How Negative Words Affect the Brain."
2. BRM Institute. 2019. "Do Words Hurt? Emotional Language and Stress Hormones."
3. Authentic Happiness. n.d. "Language Patterns Predict Heart Disease Across Counties." University of Pennsylvania Positive Psychology Center.
4. Gallup Workplace. 2024. "Employee Recognition and Workplace Engagement Report." Gallup.
5. MIT News. 2018. "Study Finds Conversation With Children Strengthens Brain Development." Massachusetts Institute of Technology.
6. PubMed. 2024. "Language Framing and Cognitive Perception Research." U.S. National Library of Medicine.
7. Hatzigeorgiadis, Antonis, Yannis Zourbanos, E. Galanis, and N. Theodorakis. 2011. "Self-Talk and Sports Performance: A Meta-Analysis." *Perspectives on Psychological Science.*
8. Wang, et al. 2019. "Neural Correlates of Self-Referential Negative Thinking."
9. Ezawa, A., and Steven Hollon. n.d. "Cognitive Restructuring in Cognitive Behavioral Therapy."
10. MacBeth, Angus, and Andrew Gumley. n.d. "Exploring the Relationship Between Self-Compassion and Psychopathology." *Clinical Psychology Review.*
11. Wang, et al. n.d. "Self-Affirmation Interventions and Behavioral Outcomes."
12. Wong, et al., n.d. "Limitations and Context Effects in Self-Affirmation Research."
13. Cohen, Geoffrey L., David K. Sherman, et al. 2024. "Self-Affirmation Interventions Across Contexts: A Meta-Analysis."
14. Stortenbeker, I., et al. 2018. "The Effect of Negative and Positive Physician Communication on Patient Anxiety."
15. LaMantia, Jean. n.d. "Exceptional Cancer Patients and the Work of Bernie Siegel."

THANK YOU FOR READING OUR BOOK!

Scan the QR code below to connect with us:

We appreciate your interest in our book and value your feedback, as it helps us improve future versions. We would appreciate it if you could leave your invaluable review on Amazon.com.

Thank you!

www.ingramcontent.com/pod-product-compliance
Lightning Source LLC
LaVergne TN
LVHW020643100826
845148LV00012B/2311

* 9 7 9 8 9 0 1 5 8 2 9 0 9 *